SCHOLASTIC
BOOKSHOP

Teaching Tricky

Science

Concepts

AGES 5 TO 11

DOUGLAS NEWTON

Teaching Tricky Science Concepts

Author
Douglas Newton

Editor
Dodi Beardshaw

Assistant editor
Joel Lane

Designer
Paul Roberts

Cover designer
Allison Parry

Cover and contents
Illustration © Colin Elgie,
Apple © Ingram Publishing,
Sky © Photodisc, Inc.

Illustrations
Andy Miles

British Library Cataloguing-in-Publication Data
A catalogue record for this book is available from the British Library.

ISBN 0-439-98448-3

© 2004 Scholastic Ltd
Text © Douglas Newton 2004

Published by Scholastic Ltd,
Villiers House,
Clarendon Avenue,
Leamington Spa,
Warwickshire CV32 5PR

Printed by Bell & Bain Ltd, Glasgow

2 3 4 5 6 7 8 9 0   5 6 7 8 9 0 1 2 3

Contents

Introduction

What this book is about

This book shows you how to help children grasp some of the harder parts of science. It is not meant to replace what you usually do in your science lessons, but to help you make the most of the topics you teach. You can use the topics exactly as they are or adapt them to suit your needs. You will find in each topic:

▶ a brief outline of the background science
▶ examples of some of the problems that children can have
▶ a way of teaching the topic for understanding
▶ some things to talk about and hands-on activities for the children to do
▶ examples of questions and tasks for checking the children's understanding.

Understanding science

The emphasis in this book is on helping children to understand science. When children understand, they make sense of the world they live in, they learn more and they can do more. At times, helping children understand is straightforward. A branch falls from a tree and bounces on wet grass. The children see the rotten wood and feel the spongy ground, and can explain why that branch fell and bounced. But some things in science can be more difficult. For example: Where did the water in that pool go? What is the difference between melting and dissolving? Where is the energy in a stretched rubber band? Why does that shadow look fuzzy? Why did that empty bottle sink? Why will the bulb not light up with just one wire? Why are such things harder to grasp than other bits of science? There are several reasons why these questions can be difficult:

▶ the children may not be able to see anything happening (as in *evaporation*)
▶ the science may involve abstract ideas (as with *energy*)
▶ there may be long chains of thought that lose children along the way (as in understanding the shadows made by a big lamp)
▶ children may bring with them ideas about how the world works that conflict with scientific explanations (as when believing that anything hollow will float).

In some topics, more than one of these may apply. For example, children may come to a lesson on electricity with the belief that bulbs consume the electricity. This may lead to the assumption that only one wire from the battery to the bulb is needed. As they cannot see an electrical current, there is nothing obvious to contradict that idea.

We can also add difficulties by the way we teach. For instance, we may:

▶ assume that children know more than they really do
▶ assume that children have a firm grasp of what they know when, in reality, they have only a tenuous hold on it
▶ think the steps we take in our teaching are small when, to a child, they are enormous leaps
▶ move on too quickly and fail to make new understandings secure.

Finally, what happens in children's minds is beyond our reach. We cannot give them our own understanding. They have to notice relationships and make connections for themselves. But we can do a lot to help them.

Supporting understanding

There are ways of supporting understanding. These include:

1 Making the invisible visible

Sometimes you can make the invisible visible, as when you hang out a wet towel on a cool day so that the evaporating water can be seen as a mist rising from the towel (see 'Evaporation', page 87). By itself, that may not be enough. You can highlight what matters by drawing attention to it, as when you say 'Look at that! What is coming from the towel? Why is it doing that? What will the towel feel like if we leave it for a long time?'

2 Tying abstract ideas to concrete objects

Energy is the capacity to do work. This is a rather meaningless statement for most children. It only replaces the word *energy* with *capacity* and *work,* and these may be just as unintelligible. However, you can show children the spring in a wind-up toy, how winding it up can change it and how it can make things move when released. The wound-up spring is ready to make the toy move. In this case, energy amounts to being wound up and ready to do something. Abstractions begin to have meaning when they are tied to specific examples.

3 Providing something to think with

Not all processes can be made visible, and some may be quite complex. In some cases, we may be able to side-step the difficulty by using an analogy. For example, when teaching about the flow of electricity through a circuit, we might draw parallels with a pump action soap dispenser. This is half-filled with water and fitted with a transparent, flexible tube that curves from the spout in a loop and returns to the dispenser through a hole in its shoulder (see page 116 in the section 'Electrical circuits'). After observing its action and trying it out, one excited seven-year-old saw the connection with his electrical circuit:

> **Child:** It's just… kind of… a bit like water. It's going round and into the bulb.
> **Teacher:** What… the electricity's like water?
> **Child:** Yes.
> **Teacher:** How's the electricity like water?
> **Child:** Because, with the pump, you press that and the water goes round, but that goes back to the bottle… Like, say that was the light bulb and this was the battery. Press that… Right? And it would go all into the battery.
> **Teacher:** So what's happening to the electricity here?
> **Child:** The electricity's going through these wires… *(description of the path of the electricity)* …Electricity just looks invisible to us.
> **Teacher:** It does?
> **Child:** You see… with water… we can see the water as it moves along.
> **Teacher:** That's right.
> **Child:** With electricity, electricity's absolutely invisible to us.

An analogy of this kind can give the children something to think with that works better than the ideas they brought to the lesson. Children can respond well to analogies provided they are familiar with what underpins them. In the case of the water circuit, this means that you should spend a few minutes demonstrating its action and letting the children have some hands-on experience first. Analogies have limitations that should not be ignored. For instance, if you cut the tube, water runs out and makes a mess. Electricity, on the other hand, does not run from a broken wire in a child's circuit.

4 Filling in the gaps

There are times when explanations leave gaps that are too big for the child to cross. We assume that the connections are obvious, so we do not state them. We may say, for example, 'So the toy car goes farther this time,' but do not add (or ask for) the reason, 'because the slope is steeper'. Some children may not fill the gap for themselves. At times, the children will need help in making these connections.

5 Finding out how the children think and working with that

Children bring with them ideas about how the world works. Sometimes these are helpful, as when a child tells you that the amount of grip a shoe has on the floor depends on the roughness of the sole and the floor. Sometimes the ideas do not fit the science so well. For instance, children may believe that all lightweight things float in water. Few give up an idea like this easily. You could begin by showing that lots of lightweight things sink. Your next step might be to pose the problem, 'Why do these lightweight things sink when those float?' You might continue, 'What's different about them? Do you think that is what matters? Let's try it and see if you are right.'

6 Talking about the science

At times, the children's grasp of a topic may not be strong. They may have understood what they did and made sense of what you said, but they may not have connected it thoroughly with what they already know. By talking with the children about the science, relating it to new events and other topics, you will knit their knowledge together and make it more durable and usable. Suppose, for instance, you have been teaching about the nature of sound and then an aircraft flies overhead, making the windows rattle. You could wait patiently until it has gone and then ensure that the children get on with their work. Or you could draw attention to the rattling and ask the children to explain it. This could lead them to think of other examples, like the time a heavy lorry drove past. You could then introduce the effect of very loud sounds on hearing. Purposeful talk can help the children to make connections, and can also indicate the quality of their learning.

Paths to understanding

These strategies are a start, but how are you to present them? One way is to think of it as taking the children along a path from what they know to what you want them to know. The steps they take have to be small enough for the children to cope with, and have to hang together so that they make sense. In effect, you form a bridge that links what the children already understand to what you want them to understand (see Figure 0.1).

FIGURE 0.1

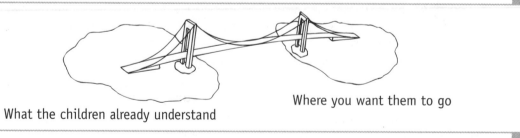

What the children already understand

Where you want them to go

Each of the topics in this book includes strategies like those above and describes a step-by-step path. What to do and what you could say in each step are described. Not all paths to understanding can be a straight line. Sometimes you may have to deal with underlying ideas first, or digress along the way. For instance, in teaching about why some things float, you may have to work on the meaning of the word *float*, the way an object pushes water aside *(displacement)* and the upward force an object experiences in the water *(upthrust)*. These could be brought together to explain why some things float and other things sink (shown schematically in Figure 0.2).

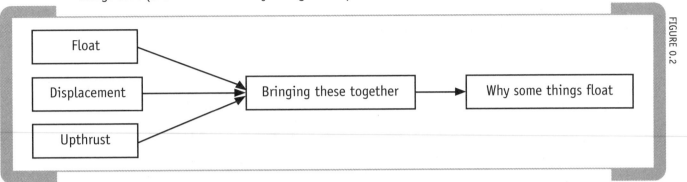

FIGURE 0.2

As a teacher, creating paths to understanding is something you do daily, often in response to the children's puzzled looks. But there are matters that are too big, too complex, or too hampered by children's misconceptions to be left to off-the-cuff responses. This book provides you with some ready-made paths to understanding, particularly for the parts of science that are often difficult to teach so that the children understand.

What you say is important

Whatever the path, what you say is very important. It involves more than merely giving instructions and telling the children what to do. Your talk should:
▶ help the children to explore their existing ideas
▶ bring out what knowledge the children will need for today's topic
▶ direct the children's attention to what matters
▶ help the children to develop and express an understanding
▶ help the children to apply their understanding.
You should not assume that the children have a good understanding just because they have finished a task or given you the 'right' answer. Talking with the children will let you know what they think. This is why the topics in this book also include suggestions for things to say. Of course, in practice, no one can predict exactly what you should say in your classroom, but it is possible to indicate its direction and general nature.

How to use this book

The topics are divided into the following chapters:
▶ *Chapter 1: Scientific enquiry* – dealing with science as a process, the scientific approach to exploration and investigation, experimenting, the testing of ideas and the nature of science.
▶ *Chapter 2: Life* – dealing with the living world and life processes.
▶ *Chapter 3: Materials* – dealing with some properties and the grouping, sorting and changing of materials.
▶ *Chapter 4: Physical processes* – dealing largely with forces, motion, energy, light, sound, electricity and the Solar System.
Within each chapter, the topics are arranged alphabetically so that you can find the one you need quickly. There is also a list of contents and a cross-referenced index to make it easier to find teaching ideas that relate to your topic. Each topic is arranged as shown in Figure 0.3.

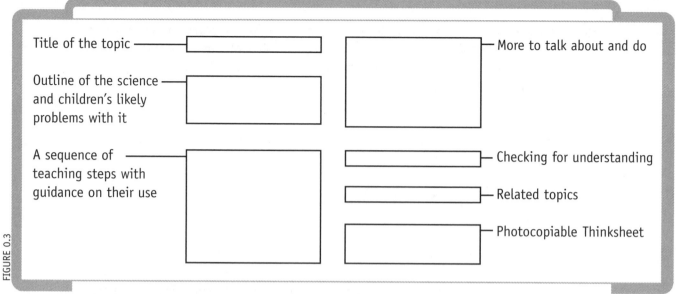

FIGURE 0.3

Title of the topic ———

Outline of the science and children's likely problems with it

A sequence of teaching steps with guidance on their use

More to talk about and do

Checking for understanding

Related topics

Photocopiable Thinksheet

Background knowledge

Each topic begins with a brief outline of the science. This summarises the main points and defines the terms. You may find this a quick way of reminding yourself of the science without having to look for it in textbooks.

Common problems with understanding

Next, you will find some of the problems children can have with the topic. This alerts you to the way they may think and respond in your lessons.

Teaching steps

After that is a set of teaching steps that form a path to understanding. Because targets and children vary, you may not need all the steps every time. You can pick and choose what you need. Advice on what is better for younger or older children is also provided immediately before the steps. Do not feel that you should cover all the steps in one lesson. In some topics, it would be more effective to teach them separately over several weeks, blended with various activities. Guidance is also provided on the likely duration of the steps. Remember that you will want to include your own written and other activities among the steps, so allow time for those too.

Suggestions for what to say and do

Talk is very important for understanding. Your part in it is critical and should not be neglected. You can never predict talk exactly, but it helps to have some ideas for your classroom conversations about science. These are provided after each step.

More things to talk about and do

Following the steps is some information that will help you to take understanding further, add an extra dimension to the work or discriminate it from other topics. While many of the earlier steps involve hands-on experience for the children, you may want more in order to consolidate and extend learning. Some suggestions are provided.

Checking for understanding

It is essential that you check on the children's understanding. It helps you to decide how effective your lesson has been, and whether you will need to do more. Asking children questions or having them do tasks can also make them think and improve their understanding. But this depends on the kind of questions you ask. If you ask only for facts, figures, descriptions and the names of things, you will help the children memorise these, but may do little for their understanding. You should also ask for explanations (in the children's own words, not yours), translations and interpretations (for example, from pictures into words and vice versa), predictions (*What will happen if…?*), reasons (*Why do you think that?*) and applications (*How can I make it…? Why will that work?*)

Related topics
There may be times when you want to relate what you are doing to another topic. A list of related topics is provided to help you identify them quickly.

Photocopiable Thinksheets
Photocopiable Thinksheets are included at the end of every chapter. These have various forms. Some are for you to use with the children as you take them through the steps. Others are for the children to work on after the steps are completed, or to support work on the additional activities. The word *Thinksheet* is used to emphasise that thinking about the science is important, as that is what can lead to understanding.

Constructing your own steps to understanding
It is not possible to anticipate every difficulty that every child will have in understanding science. There will be occasions when you want steps to help a child grasp some other topic. For that reason, a short chapter on how to construct steps for the children is provided at the end of the book.

Safety
You must at all times remember that the safety of yourself, the children and others is your responsibility. You should ensure that what you and the children do is safe and does not contravene the rules and regulations that apply in and to your school. The suggestions in this book are for guidance only. No responsibility for loss or injury occasioned to or sustained by any person or persons acting or refraining from acting as a result of the information in this book can be accepted by the author.

Chapter 1
Scientific enquiry

This section gives you some ways of helping children grasp the nature of the scientific process, the scientific approach to exploration and investigation, experimenting and testing ideas and the nature of science. Learning about science as a way of thinking and working should develop from the children's direct experience of practical work in your lessons. The topics here are not meant in any way to be a substitute for that. There will, however, be occasions when you find that some children have missed the point and seem to make no progress in their practical skills. For instance, children may persistently guess when you want them to predict what will happen; they may not grasp what you mean by 'Look for a pattern'; they may be unclear about the concept of a variable; or their investigations may not be systematic. When that happens, one of these topics could be what you need to help you move things forward. In that sense, they can be useful temporary digressions that make progress elsewhere possible.

The units in this chapter are organised alphabetically in order to make it easy to locate the one you want. Dip into them, select from them and adapt them to support your normal routine and meet the needs of the children. The table below shows where the topics are likely to be useful.

Topic	When to use the topic
Fair tests	▶ when explaining how to test ideas in science ▶ when explaining fair and unfair tests ▶ when children fail to construct a satisfactory fair test.
Patterns in science	▶ when explaining what is meant by a pattern, relationship or association in science.
Prediction	▶ when explaining the difference between predicting what will happen and guessing what will happen ▶ when helping children to express their expectations about experiments ▶ when wanting children to suggest a testable hypothesis.
Science	▶ when explaining the nature and aims of science ▶ when emphasising the importance of testing ideas.
Scientific questions	▶ when encouraging children to ask scientific questions ▶ when teaching the distinction between scientific and other questions.
Testing ideas: more than one variable to test	▶ when explaining the value of being systematic ▶ when explaining how to control variables systematically when several factors are involved in an investigation.
Testing ideas: something to compare it with	▶ when explaining how to test an idea to see whether a given change makes a difference ▶ when explaining the need for a control in certain kinds of tests.
Variables	▶ when teaching children to identify variables ▶ when teaching children to control factors that might produce an effect in an investigation.

Fair tests

What is a fair test?

When you test something, the test has to be fair. Suppose, for instance, you want a bouncy ball. You could buy a cork ball, a tennis ball or a plastic ball. Which is the most bouncy? One way of finding out is to drop them on the floor and see which bounces the highest. You take the cork ball and let it fall on a hard floor. It bounces knee-high. You take the tennis ball and drop it from the same height on a thick carpet. The tennis ball bounces to your ankle. The plastic ball is very light. Surely it will not hit the floor as hard as the others. You help it out with a bit of a throw and it bounces waist-high from the hard floor. Obviously, the plastic ball is the best – or is it? To be fair, all the balls have to be treated equally. You have to drop them in the same way, from the same height and on the same floor. Only then can you begin to believe that the bounce is due to differences between the balls and not to something else.

Understanding the concept of a fair test

It is not that difficult for children to understand the need for a fair test. Children are usually familiar with the concept of being fair (or, to be more precise, with feeling hard done by when treated unfairly). Nevertheless, children may bend the rules a little to obtain their preferred outcome – their treasured yellow ball may be given a little help on its way to the floor, for instance. But more probably, lack of experience may make children overlook sources of unfairness in their tests. For instance, they may not discriminate between a concrete and tiled floor, or not think that it matters if one of the balls is wet. You will probably need to turn some children's attention to what makes their test unfair. The aim here is to help children grasp the concepts of a fair and an unfair test.

Steps to understanding

In the steps described below, you draw on children's sense of fairness in situations they can relate to. The first three steps introduce the concept of fairness and illustrate what that means. The second step is about finding the fastest; the last step provides a new scenario that requires a fair test to find the slowest. Select the steps that are most relevant to your children's needs and abilities.

Age range and duration

If you are teaching younger children, allow up to an hour for the first three steps, ignoring time for any writing or other recording that you include. Older children will probably take these steps more quickly; but with the last step, you will still need to set aside about an hour.

Step 1: A Free Sweets Day

Tell a tale about a Free Sweets Day at the chocolate factory. All the children turn up with a bucket to collect as many sweets as possible. Sally and James go one better. Sally arrives with her bucket *and* is pushing a shopping trolley. James has his bucket *and* is wearing an enormous coat with the biggest pockets you could possibly have (see Photocopiable Thinksheet 1 on page 30). Everyone is ready for the Free Sweets Day. Discuss with the children what makes the day an unfair one and what could be done to make it fair.

> **Talk:** *Is it fair? What's unfair about it? How could it be made fair? What if everyone came with a shopping trolley?*

Step 2: Running a race

Tell the children that some people are arguing over who can run the fastest. Show the children a picture of people lined up for a race (see Photocopiable Thinksheet 1 on page 30). Some have certain advantages over others. Give the appearance of seeing nothing wrong with it. Have the children tell you what they think about it and why they think it is an unfair race.

Talk: *It looks OK to me: do you think it's not right? Why's that? What's wrong with it? How could we make it fair?* If the response is that no one should have things such as stilts or skateboards, ask: *Suppose everyone had a skateboard, would that make it fair?* The answer is, of course, that it would be fair, but we would not be finding the best runner. Ask*: What would we find out if everyone had a skateboard for the race?* (Who was the best skateboarder.) *What about the best runner on stilts? How would we do a test to find that out?* (Everyone should be on stilts.)

Step 3: The best car

Show the children a collection of toy cars. Tell them that you want to have a fair car race to find out which is the best car. First, you will have to agree on what 'best' means. (Best as the one that goes the farthest is probably the easiest concept for them to handle.) Discuss how to test the cars to find the one that goes the farthest.

Talk: *What do we mean by 'best toy car'? Is it the one that looks good or the one that goes the farthest? What do you think will help a car go a long way? Which of these cars do you think will go a long way? Why do you think that? How can we test that idea? How do we make the test fair? What should we keep the same? What will we change? How will we know which is the best car? What will that tell us about your idea about what makes a car go a long way?*

Step 4: Free fall but as slowly as possible

This is a race you would not want to win. Tell the children about an aeroplane that loops the loop. The pilot falls out of an aeroplane without a parachute. Ask how the pilot could slow her fall. What would be the best shape for her to have? (See Photocopiable Thinksheet 1 on page 30). Steer the discussion to the design of a safe, fair test. You will need drawing paper, pencils and safe scissors for the children.

Talk: *Suppose the pilot fell out of an aeroplane without a parachute. What would she do? Should she roll up in a ball? Should she spread out? Should she tuck her arms in? What do you think would be best? Why do you think that? How can we test the idea? One way of finding out what slows down the fall is to cut out matching shapes of people from paper and fold them to make the suggested postures. For example, one could be crushed into a ball and another could have its arms and legs folded in. They could all be laid on a book that is tilted, so that they all fall off at the same time. This makes it easy to see which one hits the floor last, and means that a timer is not needed.*

More to talk about and do

New Sudso

Making a fair test is one thing. Recognising an unfair test is the other side of the coin. This is particularly important if we are to avoid being misled. For example, a television advertisement might say:

New Sudso washes whiter. Look at this dirty vest. Disgusting! But when I wash it in New Sudso, see how bright and clean it is! New Sudso is better than Old Filtho. Always use New Sudso!

Ask the children whether this shows that New Sudso is better than Old Filtho. What would they do to test it properly?

Hands-on: Chocoteasers
You need some different chocolate-covered sweets (for example, Maltesers®, Revels®, Rolos®, chocolate raisins). Tell the children that you do not want to end up looking like a baby does when a baby eats chocolate. You don't even want messy hands. Do these melt in your hands? How can you compare them to find out which one messes up your hands least? Is it a fair test?

Checking for understanding
Check on the children's understanding with questions and tasks, such as:

▶ *You and your friend both have bicycles. How would you find out which was the faster bicycle?*

▶ *In horse races, the horses carry the jockeys. In some races, weights are added to the saddles of some of the horses. Why do you think they do that?*

▶ *Two girls are arguing over their pogo sticks. 'My pogo stick is better than yours!' 'No it's not!' 'Yes it is!' 'No!' 'Yes!' How will you test the pogo sticks so you can stop the argument?*

Related topics
▶ Testing ideas: more than one variable to test (page 23)
▶ Testing ideas: something to compare it with (page 26).

Patterns in science

What are patterns in science?
Scientists are particularly interested in patterns in nature – but what do we mean by *patterns* in nature? Often, things have a regularity about them. For instance, many animals have very similar structures; shadows are always on the side of the object that is farthest from the source of light; all buttercups share the same structure; light reflects off a smooth, flat mirror in a regular way; friction tends to be greater on rough, hard surfaces; and ice cubes often have a bump on the top. We can be fairly confident that these patterns will be the same tomorrow and the day after that. I would expect, for example, a ray of light to bounce off a mirror today in the same way that it did yesterday. Similarly, I would expect willow twigs to have buds dispersed along their length next year much as they were last year. Regularities like these are examples of patterns in nature. Knowing these patterns is what makes the world more predictable. Scientists note them and try to explain them.

Understanding what we mean by a pattern in science
The word *pattern* means a variety of things, even in science. Children may have met it in art as meaning a repeating design, and in craft as meaning a shape used to make identical copies or a set of instructions for making a garment. Younger children may not yet appreciate that their task in science is often to notice and learn about patterns in nature. The aim here is to help children grasp what we mean by a pattern in science.

Steps to understanding
We can help children to understand the meaning of patterns in science by beginning with physical patterns and leading them to the less obvious scientific meanings.

Age range and duration

In general, discussing the meaning of patterns in science is better suited to older children. The steps need a minimum of two hours if taught as a continuous sequence. You will probably prefer to break it into units, such as: Steps 1 and 2, Step 3, then Steps 4 and 5.

FIGURE 1.1

Step 1: Patterns around us

Have the children examine manufactured patterns, such as those: on wallpapers and fabrics, in the packaging of regular objects, in a brick wall, on a tiled roof, in mechanical structures. (See Figure 1.1.) Help them to notice the regularities and identify the repeating design in a pattern, and show them that when we know there is a pattern, we can use it to predict what things will be like elsewhere.

Talk: *Look at this piece of cloth. Which shapes happen over and over again in it? Can you find them somewhere else? Do they look the same? What's the same about them? If it happens over and over in the same way, it's called a pattern. Is this a pattern? Do you know any other patterns? Tell us about one. (Show the children part of a roll of patterned wallpaper.) What do you think the wallpaper will be like in the rolled-up part? (This is an example of how knowing the pattern helps you to predict something.)*

Step 2: Making patterns

Have the children make patterns themselves (by using potato prints, making regular structures with art straws or using regular shapes pressed into modelling clay, as in Figure 1.2). The aim is to reinforce what was done in Step 1 and let you know how well the children have grasped the concept of a pattern as a repeating design.

FIGURE 1.2

Talk: *Which shapes happen over and over again? (Or: Which shapes repeat over and over again?) Is it a pattern? What makes it a pattern? Tell everyone how you made your pattern so perfect. If you were to make a whole roll of wallpaper with your pattern, what would you have to do?*

FIGURE 1.3

Step 3: Naturally occurring patterns

Have the children look for naturally occurring patterns, such as: the growth rings in a cross-section of a tree; a spider's web; a snail shell; petals on a flower. (See Figure 1.3.) The aim is to see that there are naturally occurring patterns, but they may not always be as perfect as manufactured patterns.

Talk: *What shapes happen over and over again? Do all the leaves/snowflakes/webs/ flowers look like this? Are these patterns as 'good' as the ones you made? How are they different? Are they perfect patterns? What would they have to be like to be perfect? I wonder if the world is full of patterns. Do you know any other natural patterns? Tell us about one. What makes it a pattern? Is it a perfect pattern? What would it look like if it was perfect?*

Step 4: Patterns in what we do

Describe a behavioural pattern to the children (for example: we get up, have breakfast, go to school, have lessons and so on, repeating day after day). The aim is to widen the meaning of pattern to include non-material regularities, such as patterns of behaviour.

Talk: *There are other kinds of patterns we can look for. They are not like the ones we found on the wallpaper or the ones we made with potato prints. These are things that are the same every time they happen. Here's an example:* (a description of a behavioural pattern familiar to the children). *Are there any other patterns like this you can think of? Tell us about one. What is it that makes it a pattern? What is it that happens over and over again?* (It repeats.)

Step 5: Regularities in nature as patterns

Now have the children examine regularities in the way nature behaves (as, for example, in the way the diameter of the patch of light from a torch changes as the distance from the wall increases, as in Figure 1.4, or the way the length of an elastic band and the note it makes are related). The aim is to illustrate that regularities in nature have a variety of forms.

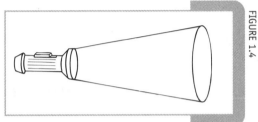

FIGURE 1.4

Talk: *What happens the same every time you do this* (move the torch away from the wall)*? What is the pattern you have found* (what is it that repeats)*? This is what scientists do: they look for patterns like these and try to explain what makes them. A scientist would notice that the circle of light always gets bigger when you move the torch away from the wall. If you were a scientist, you would think about why these things happen. Why does the circle of torchlight become bigger every time you move away from the wall?*

More to talk about and do

Patterns to talk about

Science education is intended to introduce a child to the patterns that we believe are important. When a new pattern presents itself, you might draw the children's attention to it and reinforce the message that they have found a pattern. In the meantime, here are a few patterns you might lead the children to notice:

▶ buds make a pattern along a twig
▶ the green covering on tree trunks tends to grow on the north side of the trunk
▶ the regular shapes of salt crystals.

Sometimes a pattern is not universal. Here are examples:

▶ most dogs have fur, but there is a breed of dog that has no fur (the Mexican hairless dog)
▶ water usually flows downhill, but it can go uphill (in a siphon tube).

FIGURE 1.5

Hands-on: why things fall over – finding the pattern

Give the children a tray of items, similar to those shown in Figure 1.5. Ask: *Which ones fall over easily? Why do they fall over? What kinds of things fall over easily? What is the pattern?* (Photocopiable Thinksheet 2 on page 31 accompanies this task.)

Related topics

▶ Science (page 18)

Many of the topics in this book involve seeing a pattern. For example:

▶ Changes in animals (page 42)

▶ Changes in plants (page 44)

▶ Feeding relationships (page 48)

▶ Life (page 56)

▶ Solids, liquids and gases (page 99)

▶ Gravity (page 129)

▶ Mirrors (page 136).

Checking for understanding

Check on the children's understanding with questions and tasks, such as:

▶ *In your own words, what is a pattern in science?*

▶ *Can you think of a pattern that we have not mentioned so far?*

▶ *Where is the pattern in a tomato?*

Prediction

What is prediction in science?

To predict is to say what will (or will not) happen. A prediction has to have a good reason underpinning it: it cannot be a blind guess. Usually, this good reason comes from a pattern you have noticed in the past. For example: suppose, in your experience, hollow balls have generally bounced higher than solid balls. If someone gives you another ball and you find that it is hollow, you could predict it will bounce well. The pattern you learned from your experience guides your thinking and is a good reason for your prediction. Predictions in science are important because they are involved in testing ideas. For example, experience of one sort or another gives you the idea that hollowness is what counts when it comes to bounciness in balls. You take a number of balls and sort them into those that are hollow and those that are solid. You predict that the hollow ones will bounce higher than the solid ones, all else being equal. You then test your prediction. If it comes out as predicted, you can have some confidence in your idea. This does not mean, of course, that the idea is definitely correct. Later, someone may give you a solid 'power' ball that out-bounces all the others. When that happens, you will have to modify your earlier idea or come up with a new cause of bounciness.

Understanding prediction in science

Children generally like guessing games, and can be happy using blind guesses to forecast events. They often lack the experience that makes predicting a relatively straightforward matter in everyday situations. They may even confuse guessing and predicting, treating predicting as a synonym for guessing. The aim is to distinguish between the two and lead children to make predictions in science. Having children make predictions is also a way of making them use and develop their knowledge and show you that they understand it.

Steps to understanding

The first step is to check what *guess* and *predict* mean to the children. Subsequent steps develop the distinction and use it in science.

Age range and duration

The steps are appropriate for most children except the youngest. If you use the steps with young children, you may prefer to use an explanatory expression for prediction (such as 'when you know what will happen'). You need to allow up to an hour to complete the steps, ignoring time for any writing or other child activities you include.

Step 1: Guessing

You need a marble or some similar small object to hide in your hand. You conceal the marble in one hand behind your back, then present both closed hands to the children. They are to say which hand it is in. Repeat this several times, hiding the marble at random so that there is no pattern to it and the children's response can be no more than a guess. Tie the word *guess* to the process and explain it.

> **Talk:** *Which hand is the marble in? Why do you think that? Is it just a guess? Which hand is it in this time? Was it a guess? What about now? Did you have anything to go on? Not really. It's just a guess, isn't it?*

Step 2: Predicting

Hide the marble as in Step 1, but this time establish a pattern of right hand, left hand, right hand, left hand. Now have the children predict which hand the marble will be in next. Explain how predicting is different from guessing. You can try more complex patterns (for example, one go in the left followed by two goes in the right hand, repeating this pattern).

> **Talk:** *Which hand is it in this time? Now which hand? Now which hand? Which hand do you think it will be in next time? Why do you think that? Were you right? Which hand will it be in next time? Well done! Was it just a guess? No? Do you know which hand it will be in next time? How do you know? Making a prediction is when you think you really know what will happen next.*

Step 3: Predicting the patterns on a beetle

Show a picture of a beetle with one dot on each wing (see Photocopiable Thinksheet 3 on page 32). Ask what the next beetle will be like. Ask whether this is a guess or a prediction. Show a picture of a beetle with two dots on each wing. Ask what the next beetle will be like. Ask whether this is a guess or a prediction. Continue like this:

> **Talk:** *Look at the picture of the beetle. What do you see? How many dots are there? Look at the next beetle. What's different? Tell me what the next beetle will look like. Why do you think that? Is that a guess or a prediction? Let's see if you are right. Draw me a picture of the next beetle. How do you know how many spots it will have? Is that a guess or a prediction? Was it a good prediction?*

Step 4: Practising predictions

Buds on twigs (or leaves or leaf clusters) often form a pattern along a twig. For instance, some are opposite one another and some alternate (Figure 1.6). You need some twigs with buds or leaves on them, according to the time of year. Place a bag over the top of the twig, revealing only the bottom bud. Have the children say what the next one up will be like. Reveal it and proceed. At each stage, check on the nature of the forecast (guess or prediction) by asking for reasons for the children's answers.

> **Talk:** *Can you see the bud on the twig? Point to it. What do you think the next one will be like? What makes you say that? Is it a guess or do you feel sure? Let's see if you are right. There it is. What about the next one? Are you more sure this time? So you think you know where it will be. Why do you think that?*

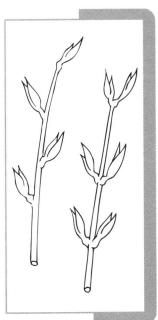

FIGURE 1.6

More to talk about and do
The aliens game
In this game, aliens step off a spaceship one by one. Each one is different. What will the next one look like? To begin with, the children can do no more than guess, but then they begin to see a pattern and use this to make predictions. Present the pictures on Photocopiable Thinksheet 3 (page 32). The children should look for a pattern and make well-founded predictions.

Hands-on: predicting how things will feel
You need a range of objects that can be handled safely, some made of metal and some of other materials – such as a scarf, a polystyrene block, a large metal spoon, a metal pencil box and a book. Metallic objects often feel cool when you touch them, because they conduct heat away from your hand. Objects made from other materials are often not such good conductors of heat, so they feel warm to the touch. Do not tell the children this pattern, but have them feel some of the items and sort them into two groups: those that feel warm and those that feel cool. Now show them some new items. Ask them to predict how each will feel. Ask them to say why they think that. This will tell you whether it is a guess or a prediction. Have the children test their predictions by feeling the new items.

Checking for understanding
Check on the children's understanding with questions and tasks, such as:
▶ *January, February, March... What will I say next? Is it just a guess? How do you know? Is it a prediction?*
▶ Show the children some elastic bands that have the same length but different thicknesses. Begin with the thinnest. How much will it stretch when you hang a weight on it? Try it, then move to the next thickness. What do they expect will happen? Will it stretch more or less than before? Can they predict what will happen with the thickest band? Is that a guess or are they sure? Ask for reasons for their answers.
▶ Let a small toy car run down a slope. Show the children a heavier toy car and let them feel the difference in weight. Now let it run down the same slope. Did it go farther than the other car? Show the children a toy car that is between the others in weight. Let them feel the car and compare it with the others. How far will it go? Why do they think that.

Related topics
▶ Patterns in science (page 13)
▶ Scientific questions (page 21).

Science

What is science?
Science provides a way of understanding the world. Possible explanations in science are tested, and those found wanting are viewed as suspect. Being a scientist means being prepared to put your ideas to the test. For example, some animals are covered in hair. Why? Is this for modesty or does it have another purpose? I notice some sheep being taken to be sheared. When they come out of the shed without their fleeces, they begin to shiver. My explanation is that hair keeps the animals warm. I think that a hot water bottle is warm like an animal, and I predict that a bottle with a hairy coat will keep warm longer than one without, all else being equal. When I test it, this comes out as predicted. The experiment did not find anything wrong with the explanation. This makes me feel more confident about it. Another scientist might disagree and say that a hot water bottle is not really like an animal. For instance, it does not have to attract a mate. Maybe hair is useful for that. More experiments can be done to test the two explanations. Eventually, scientists may agree on what animals' hair is for. As a result, the body of knowledge about living things,

materials and natural processes hangs together reasonably well and has proved very useful in technology. This does not mean, however, that this body of knowledge is fixed. While the laws, patterns and regularities in nature may not change, we can explain them in different ways, and scientists produce new ways of looking at the world from time to time.

Understanding the nature of science

A grasp of the nature of science may develop with time and experience. If that experience is biased or narrow (for instance, focusing on facts and ignoring explanations), the children may develop a conception of science that hampers their learning. Children develop conceptions of science from what they do with you, but also from what they read, what they see on television, from peers and from other adults. For instance, children may think that all scientists are old, bespectacled men surrounded by giant chemistry sets. Such beliefs place invisible limits on what children eventually do in life. Your aim should be to give the children a rich, varied and representative experience of science. The aim is to help the children develop an appropriate view of the nature of science.

Steps to understanding

Very young children do not have a clear conception of a scientist. Their conceptions begin to form by seven or eight years of age, and are well-developed by the end of the primary school. These steps are meant to help children think about what they do in science.

Age range and duration

These steps are better suited to intermediate and older primary children. The first two steps need about an hour. The final step may be taken on a different occasion, if you prefer. Allow at least half an hour for it.

Step 1: What does a scientist do?

In this step, you help the children to talk about what scientists do and to distinguish science from other activities. Encourage them to express themselves at length rather than provide only one-word or two-word answers. You could draw up 'What we do in science' and 'What we do in history' lists (and do the same for other subjects).

> **Talk:** *Do you know what a scientist is? What does a scientist do? How do you know? Can you tell me something else a scientist does? Do you all agree with that? What else? Would a scientist try to learn about animals? Plants? What about chemicals? What about the air? What about rocks? Do scientists work indoors or outdoors?*

Step 2: What are scientists like?

Have the children draw a picture of a scientist without seeing what their neighbours draw. Find out how many depict a male scientist and how many depict a female scientist. Explore the characteristics they give their scientist (for example: spectacles, bald, bearded, lab-coated). Discuss with the children how well this represents reality. Conclude by having the children draw another picture of a scientist that takes into account the discussion. Use the pictures in a 'Before' and 'After' display.

> **Talk:** *What is your scientist like? Is your scientist a man? How many drew a woman? Is your scientist old or young? Is your scientist wearing glasses? What is your scientist wearing? Where is your scientist working? What do you think made you draw your scientists like that? Are scientists really like that nowadays? How might they be different? Do they all work in special rooms called laboratories? If you were to draw another picture of a scientist, what would it be like?*

Step 3: What makes science different?

Most of the children will have been vaccinated. This provides a way into looking at Edward Jenner's experiment on smallpox (described for the children on Photocopiable Thinksheet 4 on page 33). Explore some of the key features of the experiment with the children: *What was Jenner's idea? What did he do about his idea?* Round it off with a discussion about ethical matters and how such a test would be done today.

Talk: *Who has been vaccinated? What happens when you are vaccinated? What's it for? Do you know where the word comes from? It comes from a word meaning 'cow'. What's it got to do with a cow? Here is the story of how vaccination began.* (Read the Jenner story with the children.) *Now do you see how the word was first used? In those days, many people died from smallpox. What was Edward Jenner's idea? How did he test it? What made him think his idea was a good one? Scientists have been known to try ideas like this on themselves first. Why?* (In effect, Mary Montagu 'vaccinated' her children and then hoped it had worked – copying what the Turks did. Edward Jenner vaccinated James and tested it to see if it had worked – doing an experiment. Mary's decision is quite understandable. Strictly speaking, Jenner's experiment needed another boy who did not receive the vaccination but was still infected with smallpox six weeks later. That, of course, was out of the question, even for Jenner.)

More to talk about and do

Taking on stereotypes

Talking about scientists puts the people back into science – but the scientists of the past were mostly men. You need to remind the children that things are different nowadays. Simple case studies can help to make the point. Fatima Jibrell is an environmental scientist living and working in Somalia (see Photocopiable Thinksheet 5 on page 34). You could use this story to make the point about how times have changed and continue to change.

Hands-on: a scientist 'alphabet'

Ask older children to make a scientist 'alphabet'. The children start by using books to draw up a list of as many different branches of science as they can find. Now give them sheets of A4 drawing paper. One sheet is for each branch of science. Each child or pair should write a title such as: 'Alice and Ashley are Astronomers'; 'Bishen and Bernice are Biologists'; and so on. (Two names, one male and one female, are included to make the point that both genders can be scientists. These are, of course, not necessarily the names of real scientists.) Under each title, the children should draw a picture and write a neat job description. There will be letters they will not be able to include, but they should be able to do enough to make a frieze. If you prefer, you could ask the children to write newspaper advertisements for science jobs, including brief job descriptions.

Checking for understanding

Check on the children's understanding with questions and tasks, such as:

▶ *Suppose a ship sinks when it comes into port. If this happens, there is always an investigation to find out why it sank. This involves engineers, scientists and lawyers. Some want to know who to blame. Some want to know which part of the ship broke down. Some want to know why ships like this are fine in salty seawater but sometimes sink in fresh river water. Which of these people were the scientists? Why do you think that?*

▶ *A scientist notices that dandelions close up on rainy days. She asks why, but no one seems to know. She has an idea. She thinks it might be to protect the inside of the flowers from rain so they can make more seeds. What should she do next? Think of an experiment to test her idea* (for example, compare the seeds of two dandelions, one that is allowed to open and close as normal and one that is kept open with fine wire).

▶ *People are worried that the climate will change. They think there will be less rain than there is now, and farmers will not be able to grow as much food for us to eat. A team of scientists are asked to find out whether the climate is changing. You are a member of the scientific team. What would you do?*

Related topics
▶ Scientific questions (page 21)
▶ Fair tests (page 11).

Scientific questions

What is a scientific question?

We can and do ask a lot of questions about the world and the people in it. Not all of them are scientific. For instance, we might ask someone: 'What did you say?', 'How much is that hamster?' and 'Do you think that scarf is pretty?' These are not scientific questions. That does not mean they are worthless; it is simply that they cannot be answered by science – or rather, by a scientific approach. Scientific questions are those that relate to facts and explanations about the natural and physical world and are open to practical investigation, at least in theory. Here are a few: 'How many leaves does a tree have?', 'Why does a towel soak up water but a plastic sheet will not?', 'Can a plant live without water?', 'Is all soil the same?' You could find a tree and count the leaves (or, less tediously, estimate their number). You could suggest that things soak up water if they have tiny holes in them, and test your idea. To see whether a plant can live without water, you could take two similar pot plants and water only one. After a few days, you will know whether plants need water. You could examine samples of soil from different places and see whether their composition and properties are the same. At least in principle, you could investigate each question practically.

The problem with scientific questions

Children can be very curious and ask a lot of questions. In time, however, they seem to learn that the classroom game is not about asking questions but about answering them. They can also be self-conscious about asking questions, worried that it reveals their ignorance and leaves them open to ridicule. At the same time, children are not always sure what kind of question counts in science. Their questions need to be handled with sensitivity if you want them to ask more. The aim is to encourage children to ask questions and learn what kind of questions are useful in science.

Steps to understanding

These steps are intended to help the children generate relevant questions about a given science topic.

Age range and duration

The approach will suit children of most ages; but if the children are very young, you will have to take responses orally and modify the steps accordingly. Allow at least an hour for the three steps. You will find it useful to do something with the children's questions, as suggested in 'More to talk about and do'. You will need to allow more time for this.

Step 1: Helping the children to think of relevant questions using objects

You need some trays of objects to do with your topic. For instance, if the topic were 'Seeds', you could have trays with sycamore seeds, horse chestnuts, acorns, dandelion seeds (in a plastic cup), burdock seeds and cleavers (give a firm warning about not tasting anything). After the children have had a little time to explore the objects, ask them to think about what they would really like to know about them. Give them a large sheet of paper and pencils, and have the children take turns to write their questions.

Talk: *These are some of the things we will be looking at in this topic. Have a look at them. I'll bet there's something you want to ask about them. Write it on the paper. Take turns and make me a list.*

Step 2: Helping the children to think of relevant questions using an event
A lot of children's questions are of the 'What is...?' kind. You need to encourage them to ask 'why-questions' that seek reasons for things. Use an event that has something to do with the topic. For example, in 'Stretching Things', you might show the children some tricks with a slinky spring; in a topic on 'Health', you might tell them about how you felt when you were ill; in a topic on 'Motion', you might show the children a toy car running back and forth down one cardboard ramp and up another. If the children do not respond well to begin with, try modelling what you want yourself.

Talk: *Watch this. See how the toy car goes backwards and forwards? What do you think of that? Is your thought a question? Write it down. When I see this, I wonder why the car doesn't go right up and over the top. Is there anything that makes you wonder why? Tell me what it is. Can we make that into a question?*

Step 3: Sorting the questions
Cut up the lists of questions produced in one or more of the above steps. Read each one to the children and have them sort the questions into groups. Some groups might be:
▶ We could find out by trying it for ourselves/doing an experiment.
▶ We could find out just by looking at it.
▶ We could find out by looking it up in a book/on the computer.
▶ We could not answer these questions (because...).

Talk: *Listen to this question. Is this one we can answer by trying it out ourselves or by doing an experiment? Is it one we can answer just by looking and not doing anything else? Is this one where we could find the answer in a book? So we think this is a question we can't answer in science. Some questions are like that. Why can't we answer this one in science?*

More to talk about and do
Using a Questions Box
In addition to or as a part of Step 1, put out a Questions Box and have the children write a question – something they want to know – about the topic. They can post their questions to you via the box, and you can use these to gauge their knowledge and interests. Sort and use them to make the first page of a Big Book on the topic. If the children are very young, the questions would have to be oral and transcribed by you for the Big Book.

Hands-on: answering questions
Select a question from each of the first three groups in Step 3 and ask the children to find answers. Choose carefully, so that the questions are good examples of the group and suit your resources. You will need a question that is answered by:
▶ a simple, practical test (for example, *Why do some seeds have wings?* The children drop seeds with wings and with wings cut off.)
▶ observation alone (for example, *How many seeds are there in a poppy pod?* The children shake them out and count or estimate the number.)

▶ using a book (for example, *What is it like inside our bodies?* The children find a book with a picture of a person's skeleton or internal organs.)

Checking for understanding

Check on the children's understanding with questions and tasks, such as:

▶ *Which of these questions could you answer in a science lesson?*

▶ Hold up a sheet of paper. Ask: *Think of three questions about this piece of paper for a science lesson.*

▶ *John says: 'Why did I slip? Did someone push me?' Are these scientific questions? Ask yourself, 'Does John really want to know what makes things slippery, or is he looking for someone to blame?' What do you think?* (Photocopiable Thinksheet 6 on page 35 relates to these questions.)

Related topics
▶ Science (page 18).

Testing ideas: more than one variable to test

What does testing more than one variable mean?

How to go about a test can be fairly straightforward. For instance, 'Which is strongest: the linen, cotton, polyester or nylon thread?' There are four named materials, each on different bobbins. You should take each in turn and test it, making sure the conditions are the same for them all. Similarly, 'What happens to the temperature of the soil as you dig deeper?' You should dig a spade's depth each time and take the temperature at equal intervals, measuring from the surface. Given the ability to measure depth and read a thermometer, it is relatively easy to arrive at a plan of action.

Some questions, however, are more complicated. A toy boat could have a pointed, round or flat front, and it could have a square, triangular or circular sail. Which combination makes it go fastest? The temptation is to try various combinations, more or less at random, hoping that something will come out of it. Of course, the correct approach is to test one variable at a time, keeping the other one fixed. This would mean you would take, say, a pointed boat and test each kind of sail. Then you would take, say, a square sail, and test each kind of boat. Put the answers together and you have the best combination. This way of working is systematic and time-saving.

Understanding how to test more than one variable

Children often succumb to temptation and test combinations at random. They may need help with organising their thoughts. The aim of these steps is to show them how to do this. In the longer term, the aim is for them to develop a desire and tendency to be systematic.

Steps to understanding

The point of being systematic is made in the first step. How to be systematic when testing variables is dealt with in the subsequent steps.

Age range and duration

This kind of problem is usually reserved for older primary children. Allow at least an hour for the sequence.

Step 1: Being systematic

Tell the tale of Elsa and Emma to highlight the difference between a random and a systematic approach to a problem. (See Photocopiable Thinksheet 7 on page 36.)

Elsa lost her bracelet somewhere on the school field. It was a gift from her mum and she was very upset. She just wandered around on the field looking for the bracelet, but did not find it. Emma, her friend, was more organised. She used a long rope to make a square in one corner of the field and carefully searched this square, starting in one corner and going backwards and forwards until she had finished. Then she made another square next to this one and did the same thing. 'I didn't lose it there,' complained a tearful Elsa. Emma said nothing and kept on looking, square by square, checking every part of the field until... she found the bracelet! Of course, Elsa was delighted.

Talk: *What was wrong with the way Elsa was looking for her bracelet? Elsa would have had to be lucky to find it. Why was Emma's way of looking better? Emma's way was organised and tidy. It missed nothing out. She didn't look at the same place twice, so she didn't waste time. She didn't miss anywhere. In science, you have to be organised about how you test ideas. Why?*

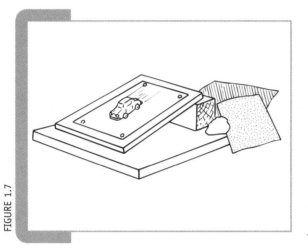

FIGURE 1.7

Step 2: What makes the toy car go faster?
Present the toy car problem to the children. You need a toy car, some modelling clay, a slope to run the car down and various kinds of paper to cover the slope. Ask: *How do we get the car to run down the slope and go as far as possible on the level?*(See Figure 1.7.) *Will the angle of the slope matter?* (You could tilt the board more.) *Will the weight of the car matter?* (You could make the car heavier with clay.) *Will the surface of the slope matter?* (You could use sugar paper or sandpaper on the slope.) *How will we find out?*

Talk: *Should we think like Elsa or like Emma? Martin was a bit like Elsa. He set up the slope, covered it with the sugar paper, put the car on it and marked how far it went. So far, so good. Then he changed the slope, put on the drawing paper and stuck a lump of modelling clay on the car, and tried that. Then he changed the slope, took off the modelling clay and tried that. What is wrong with Martin's way of working?*

Step 3: Being organised — testing one thing at a time
Write the three ideas for testing in Step 2 on the chalkboard:
▶ Will the angle of the slope matter?
▶ Will the weight of the car matter?
▶ Will the surface of the slope matter?
Discuss how to be organised about testing the car. If necessary, use the analogy of walking along a crowded pavement, using a phone, looking for a particular shop – it usually means you end up blundering into people. It is easier to stop, finish the phone call, then look for the shop. Ask the children to do one thing at a time with the car problem. Check that they keep the three tasks separate: **1** Change the slope but keep the car and surface the same. **2** Change the weight of the car but keep the slope and the surface the same. **3** Change the surface but keep the car and the slope the same.

Talk: *We think these three things will matter. What will we do? Taking one thing at a time sounds like a good idea. Well, let's give it a try. What shall we do first? How will we make it fair?*

Step 4: Bringing things together
Begin by reminding the children of the question: *How do we get the car to run down the*

slope and go as far as possible on the level? Help the children to bring their answers to the three questions together, and hence solve the problem.

Talk: *What did you find out about the first question? So the steeper the slope, the farther the car goes. What about the second question? You think the weight of the car did not matter much. What about the different papers on the slope? They did not make much difference either. Let's put them all together. For our car, the best way of getting it to run as far as possible on this floor is…*

More to talk about and do
Good thinking

To emphasise the value of being organised and doing things in the right order, talk about a factory that makes cars. Describe an assembly line. Someone has to plan it so that all the parts come together in the right order. Have the children draw an assembly line showing how they would bring things together in the right order (for example: wheels on axles, car floor, car seats, engine, steering wheel and controls, car body, lights, handles, bumpers).

Hands-on: the sinking ship

What decides how fast a ship sinks? You might introduce the problem by talking about the *Titanic*. Have the children suggest variables that may influence how fast a ship sinks. Organise their ideas in a simple picture (see Figure 1.8). One variable is fairly obvious: the size of the hole. We might reasonably expect a ship with a large hole to sink faster than one with a small hole. But do other things make a difference, such as the amount of cargo or the depth of the hole? Have the children plan and carry out an investigation to find the answer. This can be done with readily available items, such as plastic cups and marbles (see Figure 1.9). Check that their approach is systematic, and help them to bring their answers together.

I think it's the size of the hole.

I think it's how heavy the ship is.

I think it's how deep the hole is.

FIGURE 1.8

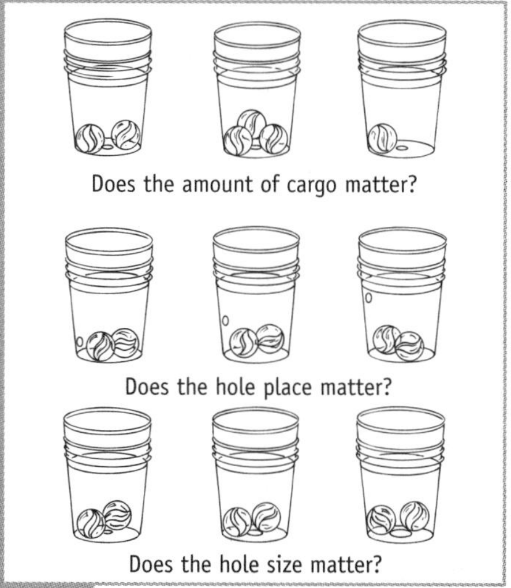

Does the amount of cargo matter?

Does the hole place matter?

Does the hole size matter?

FIGURE 1.9

Checking for understanding

Check on the children's understanding with questions and tasks, such as:

▶ *Archaeologists dig up the remains of ancient houses. Before they start, they divide up the ground into squares and draw the squares on their map. How does this help them?*

▶ *Floods! Indiana Ted is trapped! Can he escape? He needs a boat! He looks around the room and sees a pile of old newspapers, some wrapping paper and a roll of wallpaper. He knows how to make paper boats. Can he make a big boat that will last long enough to escape? Which paper should he use? Should he make a boat with a square front or a pointed front? Should the sail be square or triangular? How would you test them for him?* (See Photocopiable Thinksheet 7 on page 36.)

▶ *A toy company wants better marbles. Are big marbles better than small ones? Should they make them from glass, plastic or wood? What would you do to find out?*

Related topics
▶ Fair tests (page 11)
▶ Testing ideas: something to compare it with (page 26).

Testing ideas: something to compare it with

What is 'something to compare it with'?

Often, we want to know whether a simple change will make a difference. For example, will cress seedlings grow better on the windowsill? It would not be enough to put the seedlings on the windowsill and watch them. They may have grown just as well, or better, where they were before. The test needs a pot of seedlings on the windowsill and a matching pot on the table to compare it with. (Scientists call the one on the table the *control*.) If we are careful to make sure that these pots of seedlings are identical and we treat them in the same way – apart from where we place them – then the test will be fair. We can believe that, if the seedlings grow better on the windowsill, it is due only to their position.

Understanding 'something to compare it with'

Children may not see the need for something to compare it with unless it is pointed out to them. For example, if you ask 'Does cold tea make cress plants grow better?' they may simply water the plants with tea and judge whether it makes a difference. They do not always see that something else could change in the meantime and that this may be what makes the difference. The aim here is to help the children understand the need for something to compare a change with.

Steps to understanding

The first step is to make sure that the children know what is *not* said in comparisons of this kind. The other steps involve recognising a good test and spotting the flaw in a bad one.

Age range and duration

The sequence of steps is suitable for all but the youngest children. You will need up to an hour for them.

Step 1: Identifying what to compare it with

The conventions of language allow us to miss out the comparison. We ask, 'Will cress seedlings grow better on the windowsill?' but may not add, 'than they do on the table?' Have the children practise supplying the missing comparison to make them aware of it. (See Photocopiable Thinksheet 8 on page 37).

> **Talk:** *Glen is always asking questions but he never finishes them properly. Finish them for him.*

Step 2: Spotting a good test when they see one

Tell the children the following story and use it to explore the concept of 'something to compare it with'. In this example, there is something to compare. Angela has two babies. One is called Bobby and the other is called Duncan. They are twins and look exactly the same. She feeds them both on Lacto milk. It is good milk, but she thinks it makes them burp a lot. The advertisements say 'Easytum milk is much better'. Angela decides to try it. She gives Bobby a bottle of Lacto milk and Duncan a bottle of Easytum milk. She watches them carefully and counts their burps. Bobby burps 27 times and cries a lot. Duncan burps 9 times and smiles at her. She decides to change to Easytum milk.

> **Talk:** *Why did Angela not give both twins Easytum milk? Why does Angela think Easytum milk is better? What difference would it have made if Bobby had burped 7 times instead of 27 times?* (You may be able to use this 'twin' idea when talking of 'something to compare it with' in the children's investigations.)

Step 3: Nothing to compare it with: spotting what is wrong

Tell the children about Kamal, the keen gardener. Kamal has a row of cabbage plants and has heard that cold tea makes them grow better. He decides to try it and gives the plants cold tea every day. The weather is good for gardens. It is warm and showery. The cabbages grow well. Kamal decides that the tea idea is a good one and he will use it again next year. Discuss this with the children. Is the evidence good enough?

Talk: *What do you think? Has the tea made a difference? What else might have made the cabbages grow well? What would you do to find out if it was the tea that made the difference? How would that show you it was not the good weather that did it?*

More to talk about and do
Talking about investigations of this kind

Not all practical investigations need a 'twin' – but when they do, have the children identify the 'twin' and justify the need for it. You could do this with the next example.

Hands-on: will the flowers last longer?

Complain about how quickly flowers in a vase wilt. Tell the children: 'I've heard that if you put a teaspoon of lemonade in the water, they last much longer.' Have the children test the idea. Their test will need two flowers, a pair of matching vases containing equal amounts of water, a teaspoon and some lemonade.

Checking for understanding

Check on the children's understanding with questions and tasks, such as:

▶ *Angela's grandmother did not have a refrigerator. She kept her milk in a cool cupboard, but in summer it still went sour quickly. 'I wonder if it would last longer if I stood it in a bucket of cold water?' she thought.*
This is a bit like one of Glen's questions. Can you finish it off?
▶ *How would you test Grandma's idea?*
▶ *Why do you have to have a 'twin' bottle of milk in the cool cupboard?*

> **Related topics**
> ▶ Testing ideas: More than one variable to test (page 23)
> ▶ Variables (page 27).

Variables

· ·

What is a variable?

A variable is something that can be changed or made different. The colour, thickness and length of an elastic band are *variables*. If you were interested in what makes a band hard to stretch, these variables might make a difference.

Suppose you decide to test the effect of thickness on how hard it is to stretch a band. You have to compare like with like, so the bands will have to have the same colour and the same relaxed length. In this case, the colour and the relaxed length are known as the *controlled variables* because you controlled them (kept them the same or matched them).

You now hang something on the bands and see how far each one stretches. As you might expect, thin bands stretch more than thick bands. The amount the bands stretch is called the *dependent variable* because it depends on how thick the band is.

Finally, you chose the thicknesses to test. The thickness of each band depends on nothing other than your choice. For that reason, the thickness of the band is called the *independent* variable in this investigation.

Of course, if you decided to find out whether colour made a difference, colour would become the independent variable (you choose it), the stretch would still be the dependent variable, and the relaxed length and thickness would now have to be the controlled variables (kept the same or matched).

Understanding the concept of a variable

Children may have neither met the word *variable* nor heard it used in a scientific way. The various kinds of variable add to the children's confusion. The aim here is to help children learn about the concept of a variable in familiar contexts. They can then recall and use this in less familiar situations.

Steps to understanding

Teaching about variables is generally introduced when the children are engaged in some specific investigation. If this is unsuccessful, you could supplement the introduction with these steps and recall them in later work.

▶ The first and second steps develop the idea of variation with an example the children will know well.

▶ The third step introduces the term *variable*. It could be omitted if you think it is not appropriate for your children at this stage.

▶ The final step exercises the children's grasp of the idea in a simple context.

Age range and duration

These steps are better suited to older primary school children. Altogether, you need to set aside about an hour for the sequence.

Step 1: Something that can be different

You need a sweater as a visual aid. Through questions, explore the ways in which it could be different (for example, thicker, longer, fleecy, V-necked, a different colour). Describe these as 'things that we could make different' and 'things that we could change'.

> **Talk:** *Are all sweaters like this? How are they different? They could be longer than this one. Any other way? They could be fleecy. Anything else? They could be thicker... So sweaters can be different. They vary. Let's see if we can work out some of the different sweaters we could have (see Photocopiable Thinksheet 9 on page 38). See how the first line of sweaters varies. They change from being short to being long. What about the second one? It starts off narrow. How will it end up? What will the ones in between be like?*

Step 2: What happens when you change things

You need the sweater used in Step 1. Through questions, explore the possible effect of each variable on the warmth of the sweater. Use the terms *change* and *vary* interchangeably to help establish the meaning of 'vary'.

> **Talk:** *Why do you wear a sweater? Do you think the length matters if you want to keep warm? Do you think that how tight it is makes a difference? Do you think being warm depends on how thin it is? What about the shape of the neck, might that make a difference? Would being warm depend on the colour? Put a ring around the sweater in each line that you think would be best at keeping you warm (see Photocopiable Thinksheet 9 on page 38). Design the sweater you think would be best of all. Draw a picture of it. Use your ideas from each line of the table. So you have varied things and drawn the sweater you think will keep you really warm.*

Step 3: The naming of parts

In this step, introduce and practise the word *variable*.

> **Talk:** *We call the length of the sweater a variable. Why do you think we call it a variable? Because we can vary or change the length. What else can we vary or change? Tightness. So tightness is another...? (Variable.) Can you tell me another variable? (and so on) Invent a sentence that has the word 'variable' in it, used like this, and write it down. If you had to test sweaters to find what makes them good at keeping you warm, which variables would you test?*

Step 4: Practising in a new context

You need a toy boat to show the children. Explore with them the ways in which it could be different (for example, colour, narrowness, how heavy it is). Explore the effect of each of these on the speed of the boat in water. Have the children use whatever vocabulary you have introduced to help them respond.

> **Talk:** *Look at the boat – what could we change? What effect might that have on how fast the boat could go? Why do you think that? How would you test your idea?*

More to talk about and do

Developing relevant vocabulary

The term *variable* and its versions can be tricky for children. They need a careful and gradual introduction. In English work, explore the meanings of 'vary', 'variation' and 'variable' through words such as 'change' and 'different', and encourage the children to practise using them. When you judge the children to be ready, try introducing the different kinds of variable. 'Controlled variable' is perhaps the easiest, as it can be described as 'the thing we keep the same'. 'Independent variable' could be next, described as 'where we can choose'. Finally, 'dependent variable' can be defined as the one that 'depends on what we do'. It tends to take a lot of practice for children to understand and retain the difference between these terms.

Hands-on: gloves

Having done the sweater activity with your help in Step 1, the children should be able to attempt other versions of this activity themselves. You need a few gloves and a mitten. Use these as stimulus materials and have the children construct a chart like that on Photocopiable Thinksheet 9 on page 38 to show variables relating to glove-like attire.

Checking for understanding

Check on the children's understanding with questions and tasks, such as:

▶ *Look at this cup. Tell me one way it could be different. Draw me three pictures of cups that are all different in this way. What have you varied?*

▶ *Look at this marble. Have you seen any different marbles? How were they different? What marble variables are there? Draw me some pictures to show what these differences are.*

▶ *Look at this piece of string. How many things could we vary? What are the string variables? If you wanted a really strong piece of string, which of these might be important?*

Related topics
▶ Fair tests (page 11)
▶ Testing ideas: more than one variable to test (page 23)
▶ Testing ideas: something to compare it with (page 26).

Fair tests

Free Sweets Day

It is Free Sweets Day at the chocolate factory! Everyone is ready for the doors to open.

1 Is this fair?
2 What makes it unfair?
3 How would you make it fair?

Ready for the race

Everyone is ready for the race to find out who can run the fastest. They are all lined up at the starting post.

1 Is it a fair race?
2 What makes it unfair?
3 Would it be fair if everyone used a skateboard?
4 If everyone used a skateboard, would that tell you who was the fastest runner?
5 What would it tell you?
6 How would you find out who was the fastest runner?

Loopy Lulu

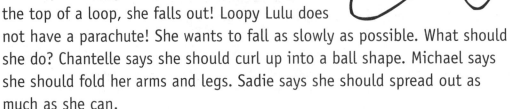

Loopy Lulu flies an aeroplane. She is a very good pilot and can make the aeroplane loop the loop. One day, when she is upside-down at the top of a loop, she falls out! Loopy Lulu does not have a parachute! She wants to fall as slowly as possible. What should she do? Chantelle says she should curl up into a ball shape. Michael says she should fold her arms and legs. Sadie says she should spread out as much as she can.

Cut out pilot shapes from paper and do a fair test to find out whose idea is best.

Why do things fall over? What is the pattern?

Patterns in science

1 What kinds of things fall over easily?

2 Try the things you have been given. As you test each one, draw it in the correct box below.

Things that fall over easily	Things that do not fall over easily

3 Have you found a pattern? What is the same about all the things that fall over easily?

4 Why are racing cars low and wide?

5 Would a tall bus with a big engine make a good racing car? Why do you think that?

Prediction

'Beetles'

The first beetle you see is like the one in the first picture. The second beetle is like the one in the second picture, and the third beetle is like the one in the third picture.

Draw what you think the next beetle will be like in the fourth box.

The aliens have landed

The aliens have landed! You see them leaving their spaceship one by one. They all look different. Can you see how they are different?

What will the next alien look like? Draw the next alien in the space where the ? mark is.

The story of smallpox and vaccinations

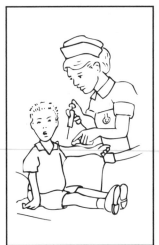

Many years ago, a disease called **smallpox** killed lots of people. There was no cure, and people simply hoped they and their children did not catch it.

Mary Montagu was the wife of the British Ambassador in Turkey. She saw how the Turks tried to protect their children against smallpox.

They did this by rubbing pus from someone who had smallpox into scratches on their own children. The children caught a mild dose of the disease. If they survived, they never caught the disease again. They were **immune**. Mary tried it on her own children and it worked. The method spread, but it was very risky.

Cows catch a disease called **cowpox**. Cowpox is like smallpox but much less dangerous. Milkmaids often caught it from the cows they milked, but the illness was mild and they soon recovered. A doctor called Edward Jenner heard a milkmaid say that milkmaids never get smallpox if they have had cowpox. Dr Jenner asked himself whether infecting people with cowpox would be a safe way to protect them from smallpox.

To test his idea, he infected a young boy called James Phelps with cowpox. Six weeks later, after James had got over the cowpox, he tried to infect James with smallpox. Fortunately for everyone, James did not catch that terrible disease. He was immune. Dr Jenner had **vaccinated** James. Since then, **vaccination** has helped to stamp out smallpox all over the world.

Times have changed and science has changed with them. Today, Dr Jenner would not be allowed to test his idea in the way that he did. What if the test had shown that

Edward Jenner

his idea was wrong? James would be dead! Today, ideas are looked at very carefully before they are tried on people.

1 What was Dr Jenner's idea?
2 What did he do to see whether it was a good idea?
3 Why was Dr Jenner's way of testing his idea better than Mary Montagu's way?
4 Dr Jenner's way of testing his idea was not perfect. How was it not perfect?

What does a scientist do? (2)

Fatima Jibrell: a scientist who looks after the world around us

There is a country in East Africa called Somalia. Changes in the weather are making the deserts spread, and wars have made things worse. This is Fatima Jibrell's country. She grew up there and can remember what it was like when she was small. There were flowers and trees and water for the animals. There were even lions, and she can remember how her mother had to tie her on a rope so that she would not wander from the safety of the camp. But now the trees are gone. Where there was grass, there is now dry dust.

Fatima grew up and went to America to study how we can take care of the land. Now that she is back in Somalia, she is trying to make things better. The people need land and water to grow food and to drink. They should not cut down the few trees that are left, and should plant more.

It is not easy for Fatima to get people to change their ways. Women are not listened to like men, even when what they say makes sense. But if scientists like Fatima can change the way people think, then trees and other plants will grow again and life for the Somalians could be better.

Answer these questions on another sheet of paper.

1 Why have the animals died or gone away?
2 People do not eat trees, so why is planting more trees a good thing in Somalia?
3 What else might the Somalians do to make things better?
4 Do you think it will be hard or easy for Fatima Jibrell to change what people do?
5 Why do you think that?

A question of science

Here is a list of questions.

1 Put a tick next to the ones you think could be answered in a science lesson.

2 Write a sentence to tell me why you think each one is a good science question. Write on the back of this sheet.

a) Why did the boat sink?   b) Which king did that?

c) How many petals does a rose have?

d) Was it only rich people who had nice clothes in those days?

e) What is the best way of getting sand out of my clothes?

f) What part of the world did it come from?

g) Why is a hawk's beak hooked?   h) How do I make a cake?

i) How can I draw a dog?   j) What do hedgehogs eat?

Inventing questions

Look at the paper this is written on. Feel it.

Think of three questions about this piece of paper for a science lesson. Write them here.

1 _____

_____

2 _____

_____

3 _____

_____

Curiosity or blame?

John was standing in a line with his classmates. He fell over. John says: 'Why did I slip? Did someone push me?'

Are these scientific questions? Ask yourself, 'Does John really want to know what makes things slippery or is he looking for someone to blame?' If he wants to know why some things are slippery, it is a scientific question. If he wants to blame someone, it is not. What do you think?

Scientific questions

Finding Elsa's lost bracelet

The first picture shows how Elsa wandered around the field looking for her bracelet. The second picture shows what Emma did. She made square shapes on the field and searched in each square, one after another, like the picture shows.

How Elsa looked

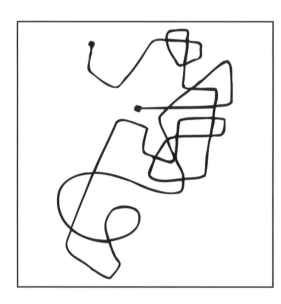

How Emma looked

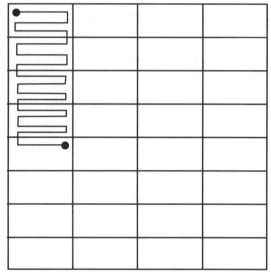

1 What was wrong with the way Elsa was looking for her bracelet?
2 Why was Emma's way of looking better?

The adventures of Indiana Ted

Floods! Indiana Ted is trapped! Can he escape? He needs a boat! He looks around the room and sees a pile of old newspapers, some wrapping paper and a roll of wallpaper. He knows how to make paper boats. Can he make a big boat that will last long enough to escape?

1 He has newspaper, wrapping paper and wallpaper. Which paper should he use?
2 He can make a boat with a square front or a pointed front. Which shape should he make?
3 He can have a square sail or a triangular sail. Which sail should he use?
4 Invent an experiment to find out what kind of boat Indiana Ted should build. Write about what you would do to find out, so you could let him know the answer by telephone.

Testing ideas: more than one variable to test

Glen's questions

Glen is always asking questions, but he never finishes them properly. Here is one of his questions:
'Will our cress plants grow better on the windowsill?'
What he really means is:
'Will our cress plants grow better on the windowsill than on the table?'

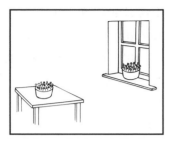

Here are some more of his questions. Finish them for him by writing on the line at the end of each question.

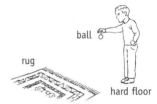

1 Will the ball bounce better on the hard floor?

_____

2 Will a conker be harder if I soak it in salty water?

horse chestnuts

_____

3 Will these new shoes help me jump higher?

_____

4 Will a sweet last longer if I break it into little bits, then put all the bits in my mouth at once?

_____

5 Will the cakes be bigger if I put an extra spoonful of sugar into the cake mix?

_____

6 Will plant food make plants have more flowers?

_____

Testing ideas: something to compare it with

Ways in which sweaters can be different

Sweaters can be different. They can be:
- short or long, or any length in between
- tight or loose, or anything in between
- thin or thick, or anything in between
- V-necked or polo-necked, or some other shaped neck
- red or blue, or some other colour.

1 In the empty boxes, draw sweaters that vary between the labels in the first and last columns. The first one has been done for you.

short			long
tight			loose
thin			thick
V-necked			polo-necked
red			blue

2 What kind of sweater do you think will be best for keeping you warm?

3 Design a warm sweater. Think about ways that sweaters can be different. Put together the things that might make it warm in your design.

4 Draw your warm sweater on the back of this sheet.

Variables

Chapter 2
Life

This chapter gives you ways to help children grasp aspects of the living world and life processes. It deals with teaching about life, animals and plants, food and feeding, and some systems and senses of the body. It includes topics on changes in animals and plants. Further topics to do with changes will be found in Chapter 3 – and you may prefer to bring these together, according to how you want to teach them. The topics in this chapter are organised alphabetically to make it easy to locate the one you want. Use them to support your normal routine when teaching science. Dip into them as you need. The table below shows where the topics are likely to be useful.

Topic	When to use the topic
Animals	❥ when teaching about the characteristics of animals and what they have in common ❥ when explaining that humans are animals ❥ when describing similarities and differences between humans and other animals.
Changes in animals	❥ when teaching about changes over time (see also Chapter 3) ❥ when teaching about life cycles ❥ when explaining adaptation in animals.
Changes in plants	❥ when teaching about changes over time (see also Chapter 3) ❥ when teaching about life cycles ❥ when explaining adaptation in plants.
Digestion	❥ when explaining why we eat ❥ when describing what happens to food ❥ when explaining nutrition.
Feeding relationships	❥ when explaining the relationships between living things in their environments ❥ when explaining why we need to care for and protect the environment ❥ when explaining the nature of food chains and food webs.
Green plants	❥ when teaching about the characteristics of plants ❥ when explaining the needs of plants ❥ when teaching about the parts of plants and their functions ❥ when describing growth and explaining nutrition in plants.
Hearing	❥ when explaining the senses ❥ when teaching about sound (see also Chapter 4) ❥ when explaining that sounds are vibrations transmitted through the air.
Life	❥ when teaching about the characteristics of life ❥ when teaching about the distinction between living, once-lived and never-lived.
Microbes	❥ when teaching about the variety of life ❥ when explaining the meaning of health and illness ❥ when explaining the need for hygiene ❥ when describing beneficial and harmful micro-organisms.
Plant food	❥ when explaining that plants do not eat or take in food like us but make their own ❥ when explaining plant nutrition ❥ when teaching about the role of the leaf and root.
Seeing	❥ when explaining the senses ❥ when teaching about light (see also Chapter 4) ❥ when helping children understand that eyes do not emit light in order to see.
Skeleton	❥ when explaining the functions of the skeleton ❥ when teaching about animal movement.

Animals

What are animals?

Animals come in all shapes and sizes. Many are very simple – such as the amoeba, which consists of only a single, tiny cell. Others, such as people, are much more complex. They have body cavities and a supporting skeleton. Animals have some sort of covering, such as skin, over which may be another covering, such as fur, feathers or scales. Most animals can move bodily from place to place, though they have different ways of moving. For instance, some walk, some fly and some swim. None can make their own food in their bodies, so they all have to take food in. Animals also breathe, sense their surroundings, reproduce and excrete waste materials.

Understanding animals

Children tend to subdivide the animal world in a different way to scientists. For example, children may think in terms of: people (as a 'special' group), animals (for example, dogs, cats, horses, mice, elephants, bears), birds, fish, flies, butterflies and creepy-crawlies. For some children, people are not animals. The aim here is to widen the meaning of 'animal' and clarify some of its important sub-groups.

Steps to understanding

You will need to remember that the following steps increase in difficulty. These steps are, of course, only the start. Follow-up work will consolidate and develop the children's learning.

Age range and duration

Young children could take the first three steps, but later steps are better kept for older children. The first three steps need about an hour and a half. The last two steps could take another hour.

Step 1: Alike and different

Here, you prepare the children for the steps to follow by having them compare and contrast some familiar animals, such as pets. Ask about how these are the same and how they are different.

Talk: *Who has a pet? What is it? Who else has a pet? What is your pet? Can anyone tell me one thing that is the same about these pets? Anything else? Do they both need to eat? What else do they both do?* (Show pictures of two pets, such as a dog and a hamster.) *These two animals have things that are the same. What are they? What is the difference between them?* (Continue with one or two other pets or familiar farm or wild animals.)

Step 2: We are animals

Have the children examine a range of animals and look for things the animals have in common. (You could use Photocopiable Thinksheet 10 on page 69 for this. The animals are arranged in a sequence that makes spotting similarities easier. This is to help you make the point that people are animals too.)

Talk: *Look at the person and the chimpanzee. What is the same about them? They are standing on two legs. They've both got two arms and two legs... Now look at the chimpanzee and the bear. What is the same about them?* (Continue through the animals, comparing them in pairs. Finally, complete the circle by comparing the fly and the person.) *Is there anything about the fly that is like the person? Both have heads. Both have legs. Anything else? So they're all a little bit like one another. Is a dog an animal? What about a bear? What about a chimpanzee? What about a person? What about a squirrel...? Are we animals too?*

Step 3: We are different
Repeat the procedure used in Step 2, but look for differences between the pairs of animals. This is to help you establish that we are all animals, but different animals.

Talk: *So we are all animals, but we are all a bit different.*

Step 4: Groups of animals
This step divides the animals into some of the familiar scientific groups: mammals (on Photocopiable Thinksheet 10 on page 69, from the person anticlockwise to the bat), birds, fish, reptiles and insects. You could tell the children what the groups are and then discuss the differences between the groups. Afterwards, the children should be able to add another example to each group on the sheet.

Talk: *Is a bear more like a dog, or is it more like a fly? Is it more like a snake or a bird? A bear is more like a dog than any of these. We are more like a chimpanzee than a lizard or a snake. Even a squirrel is more like a bear than a fly. People, bears, dogs and squirrels are a special group of animals called mammals. Mammals usually have hair or fur. Have I missed any mammals? Can you tell me the name of another mammal?* Continue like this to introduce other groups, such as birds and fish.

Step 5: Special cases
Some animals can be very difficult to fit into a group. Should the bat, for instance, be placed with the mammals or the birds? We have placed it with the mammals because it gives birth (does not lay eggs), it suckles its young and it is covered in fur (not feathers or scales). Some special cases are worth talking about, as they can help to clarify the groups. The whale is an example. It was once a land mammal, but now lives in the sea like a fish. Nevertheless, it is not a fish because it gives birth and suckles its young. It has, however, lost its fur. The seal is another mammal that lives in the sea, but it has not lost its fur. Penguins spend a lot of time in the sea and can swim well, but they are still birds.

Talk: *Why do you think I said that the bat is not a kind of bird? What about a penguin? Penguins cannot fly. Are they fish? Are they birds? Why do you think that?* (Continue like this for the seal and the whale.)

More to talk about and do
Variety, the spice of life
Talk about the advantages of variety. Ask what it would be like if all animals were the same. We would all want the same places to live, and we would all want the same food. Just think if every fly wanted a house like yours. What if the supermarket was full of horses and cows wanting to buy the same food as you? Being different means that we can all live together.

Hands-on: using keys to classify animals
Begin with a key that identifies common, everyday things. Sorting plastic cutlery is a good thing to start with. After that, have the children classify larger animals (from pictures) and then some common birds. Finally, let them try a key for classifying common insects.

There are keys readily available for children to use in identifying animals in their science books. Photocopiable Thinksheet 10 on page 69 gives the children some simple practice to prepare them for the real thing.

Related topics
▶ Green plants (page 51)
▶ Life (page 56)
▶ Skeleton (page 66).

Checking for understanding

Check on the children's understanding with questions, such as:
▶ *Are you an animal? What makes you think that?*
▶ *Is a spider an animal? Why do you think that?*
▶ *How can you tell an animal from a twig?*

Changes in animals

What are changes in animals?

Animals change with time. They grow, die and decay. In the meantime they reproduce, their offspring do the same, and so the pattern repeats itself. These patterns are often called life cycles. For example, a butterfly egg hatches, the caterpillar feeds and grows, pupates and becomes a butterfly. This butterfly mates, lays eggs and dies. These eggs hatch and the cycle continues. Similarly, a frog's egg hatches and frees a tadpole. The tadpole grows into a frog, which mates and lays more eggs. In our case, we are born, become adults and eventually die. Before that happens, we may have children who, in turn, may become adults and have children of their own. There are many kinds of life cycle in the natural world; some are simple and some are more complex.

Understanding changes in animals

Generally, young children readily accept that animals develop with time; but they may be vague about continuity and pattern during change. The aim here is to help them grasp the repeating nature and variety of life cycles and the continuous nature of change.

Steps to understanding

These steps use the children's knowledge of changes in familiar animals, such as pets and people, and draw attention to aspects of change that can slip past their attention. Then changes in less familiar animals are introduced.

Age range and duration

This sequence of steps is suitable for younger children. It could take up to three hours to complete, and longer if you include some direct observation of caterpillars.

Step 1: Growth in animals

You will need pictures of common pets, such as pups and adult dogs, kittens and adult cats. The aim is to match the young with the mature animal and have the children think about what happens in between.

Talk: Show a picture of, say, an adult dog and ask: *Do you know what this is? Is it a baby dog? How do you know it's not a baby dog? What do we call a baby dog? What do they look like? Find me the picture of a puppy. How is it the same? How is it different? How does it get to be a big dog? Does it just wake up one day like a big dog with big teeth and long legs? What happens? Does it grow quickly?*

Step 2: Steady development in ourselves

You will need pictures of a person at various ages so that they form a progression. Mix them up. Have the children help you to sort the pictures into a sequence that reveals the continuous nature of change.

> **Talk:** *Oh, dear! My pictures are mixed up. Will you help me put them in order? Where shall I start?* (The children help organise the pictures so that they form a sequence from childhood to maturity.) *Look at how X has changed! What is different? What has stayed the same? I think there is one missing from here. What would it look like? Draw me a picture to show me. My pictures end when X was just grown up. What do you think X would look like if there was another picture? Draw me a picture to show what X would look like next. Tell me how you decided X would look like that.*

Step 3: Continuous development in other animals

You will need pictures of a variety of young and mature animals. The aim is again to match the young with the adults. Then focus on one animal and have the children help you construct a sequence between the young and the mature animal reminiscent of the pictures of a person in Step 2. Of course, not all change is simply as before but bigger. For instance, elephants grow tusks and male lions develop manes.

> **Talk:** Show a picture of, say, a mature lion and ask: *Do you know what this is? Is it a baby lion? How do you know it's not a baby lion? Show me the picture of a baby lion. How is it the same? How is it different? Look, all my pictures are mixed up. Let's sort them. We'll put the grown-up there and find the baby that goes with it.* (Proceed in this manner until the pairs are complete.) *Which one do you like the most? This one? Why do you like the giraffe the most? Here's the baby giraffe. What will it look like next week? Watch, I'll draw it. What do you think it will look like the week after? I'd better draw another picture.* (Continue to adulthood.)

More to talk about and do

Other kinds of changes

Talk with the children about non-uniform changes. For instance, children grow to adulthood and then their height stays much the same for many years. There are also seasonal changes. For example, birds moult, dogs and cats shed fur, spiders and snakes shed their skins. In really cold places, hares change colour and become white to match the snow.

Hands on: watching for changes in animals

Show the children some of the changes involved in the life cycle of an animal. You may be able to collect two or three cabbage white caterpillars from cabbage or cauliflower plants in a garden. Take some of the leaves for the caterpillars to eat. Keep them in a plastic aquarium with a lid. The children can watch and record the caterpillars' development, hopefully until they pupate. Remove limp leaves regularly and replace them with fresh ones. This is obviously season- and time-dependent, so you may have to rely on a videotape or on pictures of similar life cycles to show all the stages.

Checking for understanding

Check on the children's understanding with questions and tasks, such as:
▶ *This is a baby giraffe. What will a grown-up giraffe look like? Why do you think that?*
▶ *This is a grown-up cow. Draw what it looked like before it grew up. Why do you think it looked like that?*
▶ *This is a baby bird. What will change as it grows up?*
(See Photocopiable Thinksheet 11 on page 70 for support with these questions.)

> **Related topics**
> ▶ Changes (page 80)
> ▶ Changes in plants (page 42).

Changes in plants

What are changes in plants?

Plants change with time. They grow, and many produce flowers and make seeds that disperse. Eventually the plant dies and decays. If the seeds have the right conditions, they germinate and grow and the cycle starts again. There are several kinds of cycle. Poppies, for instance, grow, flower, produce seeds and die within one year. These are annuals. Dandelions, however, grow year after year, producing flowers and seeds almost every year. These are perennials. Foxgloves, on the other hand, take the first year to grow and establish themselves but do not flower until the second year. After that, they die. These are biennials. Some plants, like the sycamore tree, lose all their leaves in the autumn. These are deciduous plants. Others, like conifers, keep their leaves over the winter and are evergreen.

Understanding changes in plants

Plants often look much the same for relatively long periods and then bloom quickly. Young children may not connect the flowering plant with what it was before or after. In effect, they see them as different plants. Growth from seeds may also be a new experience for the children. The aim here is to develop that experience, and so bring some changes in plants to the children's attention.

Steps to understanding

Growing things for the classroom needs preparation. Generally, you should allow some ten days for germination and signs of green to develop. Other plants could be substituted for those mentioned below.

Age range and duration

This sequence of steps is suitable for younger children. It involves observing and measuring plants as they grow, so the steps need intermittent attention spread over several days.

Step 1: Observing plant growth

You will need a plotted plant for the children to observe and measure. Alternatively, you could sow some lawn seed in a tray of potting compost and bring it into the classroom when it begins to grow fairly strongly. The aim is to help the children notice the slow but relatively continuous changes that take place.

> **Talk:** *What is this? What was it like yesterday? Will it stay like this? What do you think it will be like tomorrow? Let's measure it. How could we see tomorrow if what we think is right? What do you think will happen if we leave it for a long time?*

Step 2: Is plant growth the same all over the plant?

You will need access to a long-stemmed flowering plant. Daffodils growing in a pot or a dandelion plant outside are suitable. Have the children make marks with a felt-tipped pen at 1cm intervals along the stem of the flower. (Leave the flower attached to the plant so it can continue to grow.) Each day, have the children examine the stem to see what has happened to the spacing. The stem does not grow equally along its length.

> **Talk:** *What has happened? Where has it grown the most? How do you know that?*

Step 3: Growing things from seeds

This step extends over a period of time in which changes in a plant can occur. It provides an opportunity to observe at least a significant part of a plant's cycle of life. You need some plant seeds that flower fairly readily, such as Virginian stock, pansies or sweet peas. You may like to have a pot of these that have already germinated ('one I prepared earlier'). Photocopiable Thinksheet 12 on page 71 can help with this step.

Talk: (Show the children the packet of seeds.) *Do you know what these are? What do you think is inside the packet?* (Reveal the seeds and let the children examine some with a hand lens.) *What do we do with them to help them grow?* (Together, prepare a seed tray and then plant, dampen and cover the seeds. After 8 to 10 days, the seedlings should begin to appear. Ask the children to look closely.) *What can you see? What has happened to the seeds? Will they be different tomorrow?* (The children could keep a pictorial record of the seedlings' growth and flowering. If insects have access to the flowers, seeds may develop. This completes the life cycle.)

More to talk about and do
Plant catalogues and seed packets
Older children can benefit from a discussion about the information in plant catalogues and on seed packets. You can explain that plants also have Latin names, so that people anywhere in the world can know which plant we are talking about. Often there will be information on the conditions that favour particular plants. This can lead to investigations to find out the best conditions for the growth of cress seedlings.

Hands-on: an investigation to find the best place to grow some cress
Have the children sow equal numbers of cress seeds in identical plastic pots of potting compost and cover them with a sheet of card until they germinate. The problem is: *Where is the best place for these to grow? What is likely to be a poor place?* The children can test their ideas in a controlled way, using the pots of seedlings.

Hands-on: collecting, classifying and testing seeds
In the autumn, there are fruits and seeds to collect – but remind the children that they should not taste these, as some may be poisonous. Seed dispersal and how it benefits a plant can be discussed. The children can test how effective dispersal is, using winged seeds dropped from various heights.

Related topics
▶ Changes (page 80)
▶ Changes in animals (page 42).

Checking for understanding
Check on the children's understanding with questions and tasks, such as:
▶ *What happens to a plant in winter? Why do you think that happens?*
▶ *Why does a plant need its seeds to blow a long way away?*
▶ *Why do lots of plants have flowers?*

Digestion
. . . .
What is digestion in humans?
Digestion in humans takes place in the mouth, gullet (oesophagus), stomach, and gut (small and large intestines). The purpose of these parts is to process food so that useful substances can be absorbed and stored by the body. Processing begins in the mouth with saliva and continues in the stomach and gut. The useful substances we absorb provide a source of energy and a supply of materials to help make and repair body tissue. Unwanted substances are excreted.

Understanding digestion in humans

Very young children may think of their torsos as hollow receptacles for food. Older children have generally refined this view to include a stomach in the hollow receptacle. They usually know that this stomach is connected to the mouth by a tube, but they may not distinguish between the windpipe and the gullet. They often know of the gut, but are unsure of its function and how it relates to the stomach. They tend to think that the processing of food takes place only in the stomach. The aim here is to help the children grasp the structure of the digestive system and the functions of its various parts.

Steps to understanding

In anatomical drawings and models, the digestive system looks very complex. This is because there is a lot of it packed into a small space. You cannot, of course, show children human digestion in action, so the steps below set out the structure of the digestive system and then describe what each part does, using simple analogies.

Age range and duration

The steps are suitable for all children, though you may wish to simplify the robot analogy for younger children. Allow up to an hour for each step, ignoring time needed for written or other work that you add.

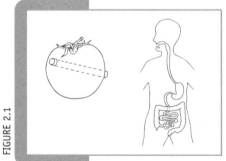

FIGURE 2.1

Step 1: The structure of the digestive system

Prepare a large outline diagram of the human body. On it, draw the digestive system, piece by piece, through discussion with the children as shown in Figure 2.1 (or more simply). Draw their attention to the way that the digestive system is essentially a tube that passes right through the body, like a plastic straw stuck through a tomato. This tube is different from the one in the tomato because liquid can soak through the tube wall.

Talk: *Where does the food go when you eat it? Let's start with your mouth. What do you do with the food in your mouth? You chew it and break it up into small pieces. Then what happens to it? It goes down your throat, then what? Into your stomach, splash – the stomach's like a bag with stomach juices in it. After it's been in your stomach for a while, where does it go? Into your gut, along the tube, and out the other end. Look at this tomato. I'm going to push this plastic straw through it and snip off the ends. How is this a bit like us? If this tomato was a person, that would be its bottom. What would the other end be?*

Step 2: What the parts do – an analogy

Take each part of the system in turn and describe what it does. Start with the mouth. Teeth break up food into smaller pieces to make it easier to digest. Saliva mixes with it and starts to break the food down into substances the body can absorb. It also lubricates the lumps of food, so they go down the gullet more easily. In the stomach, there are liquids that break the food down a lot more. When the stomach's lower valve opens, the sloppy mess goes through into the gut tube where dissolved things that our bodies need soak through into the waiting blood vessels. The blood carries what our bodies need to all parts of the body. Farther down the gut tube, water is taken out of the broken-up food and recycled.

It can help to compare this with a robot that processes food, but does not have a digestive system like ours. Give the children a copy of Photocopiable Thinksheet 13 (page 72) and talk it through. At the beginning of the conveyor belt, there are things that contain useful bits from the robot's point of view – like food for us. These items begin to be broken down into their parts by a hammer – like the action of teeth. They pass along the belt, where they are sprayed with oil to loosen the nuts and bolts. This makes it easier to break them up a bit more – like what happens in the stomach. After this, the robot picks out the bits and pieces that are useful, such as replacement parts and batteries, and fits them. This is like what happens in the early part of the gut. Further along the belt, surplus oil is removed in order to use it again – like the water taken from the waste in the gut. Finally, the unwanted parts fall from the belt into the bin – with obvious parallels.

A simplified version of this for younger children would be to omit the conveyor belt, 'feed' the robot directly and discuss what the robot would have to do to process the 'food' inside it: break it up, choose and use the bits it needs, and discard the rest.

Talk: *Look at this poor robot! It can't digest food like us. Instead, it has do its digesting on the outside. Let's see how it does it. Start at this end. Robots don't eat the same food as us. What bits do you think they need? You don't get those kinds of things in sandwiches! The bits they need are in computers and televisions and things like that. 'Yummy!' says the robot as a computer goes on to the conveyor belt. What part of us is this end of the conveyor belt like? That's right, it's like having a mouth. What happens next? The hammer breaks the computer into small pieces. Do we have anything that does that? Now oil is sprayed on the bits. What do you think it does?* (And so on, following the action in the picture to its conclusion.)

Step 3: System malfunction

Consolidate the children's knowledge of the digestive process by drawing attention to what happens when there are faults. Talk about what happens when we swallow things without chewing, and when we get a stomach infection or 'tummy bug'.

Talk: *What sometimes happens when you eat your food too quickly? Big lumps go down and you can feel them. Where do you feel them? Sometimes it helps if you have a drink of water. Why does that help? Sometimes you get infected, buggy food in your intestines. When that happens, your intestines try to get rid of the buggy food as fast as they can. What do we call that, do you know?* (Diarrhoea.) *If that happens, do you think the intestines have time to reclaim the water? What makes you think that? Why should we drink more water when we have diarrhoea?*

More to talk about and do

Getting rid of waste materials

We get rid of waste in several ways. Children tend to think only of urine and solid waste. We also get rid of waste in sweat and even in breath. We generally think of waste materials as offensive – which is just as well, because they can contain harmful microbes. This provides a good way into talking about the need for personal hygiene, hand washing after toilet use, ways of avoiding illness and the contamination of food, utensils and surfaces.

Hands-on: modelling the digestive system

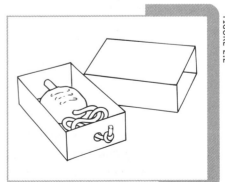

FIGURE 2.2

We began by simplifying the digestive system to a tube. Now is the time to restore some complexity to its organisation. Give the children some string to make an intestine, a small jelly sweet as a stomach and half a matchstick as a gullet. They are to pack these into a matchbox to simulate the way they are packed in the human body, and still leave space for other organs, such as the heart and lungs (see Figure 2.2).

Another way of doing this with the whole class is to fix a very

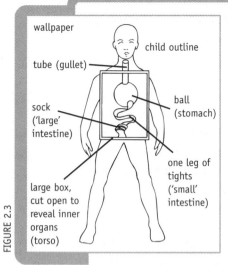

FIGURE 2.3

wallpaper

child outline

tube (gullet)

ball (stomach)

sock ('large' intestine)

one leg of tights ('small' intestine)

large box, cut open to reveal inner organs (torso)

large sheet of paper to the wall, stand a child beside it and draw around him or her to make an outline of the body, then fix objects on the outline to represent parts of the digestive system (see Figure 2.3).

Checking for understanding

Check on understanding with questions and tasks, such as:

▶ *Imagine that you take a bite of an apple. Tell the story of what happens to the piece of apple.*

▶ *Why should we chew food well?*

▶ *Why are we sometimes sick (vomit)? It seems a waste of food. What good does it do?*

Related topics
▶ Life (page 56)
▶ Microbes (page 58)
▶ Plant food (page 61).

Feeding relationships

What are feeding relationships?

You might find a frog, a flag iris and a moth in or over a pond. The iris needs air, sunlight and nutrients in the mud. The moth sips nectar from the iris flower. The frog flicks out its tongue and eats the moth. Together they form a *food chain*. The frog eats the moth, which takes nectar from the iris, which draws on air, sunlight and nutrients in the mud. There are other food chains in the pond. There may, for instance, be a fish that seeks out grubs that feed on rushes that rely on sunlight, air and nutrients in the mud. Animals cannot make their own food, so they eat other animals (frog eats moth) or plants (grub eats rush). Most plants, on the other hand, make what they need for themselves. Together, the plants and animals in this pond form a community. They depend on one another and, ultimately, on the sun's energy. Take away a part of the community and the rest may not be able to survive. On a larger scale, we could think of all life on the planet as being interdependent like this. Damage a part of it too much and a food chain, or even the whole community, may collapse.

Understanding feeding relationships

Children's experience of the ways living things relate to one another in feeding patterns is limited. They may be able to identify a predator and its prey in some instances (such as a fox that takes a chicken), but they tend not to see the bigger picture. Nor do they see the pattern repeated in other habitats. The aim here is to help them identify feeding patterns and recognise them elsewhere.

Steps to understanding

This sequence of steps can be used with any habitat (for example, a pond, a hedgerow, the seashore). It assumes you have already made the children familiar with the main animals and plants in the habitat.

▶ Step 1 prepares the children for an analogy.
▶ Step 2 introduces the children to food chains in a habitat.
▶ Step 3 uses the analogy to look at a food chain.
▶ Step 4 is relevant when you introduce a new habitat.

Age range and duration

Not counting what you did to introduce the animals and plants of the habitat, the first three steps need at least an hour. The final step adds another fifteen minutes, but is only relevant when you compare communities of plants and animals in different habitats. All steps are appropriate for all but the youngest children.

Step 1: The tale of the Giant Sherbet Eater

Tell the story of the Giant Sherbet Eater. This is a specialised animal that eats powdered sherbet via its straw-like mouth. A bun or cabbage would be no good. It cannot make its own sherbet, so depends on sherbet-makers and sugar-growers. Together, they form a chain: Sherbet Eater – sherbet-maker – sugar-grower – sugar fields. As there are lots of fields, many sugar-growers, fewer sherbet-makers and only one Sherbet Eater, they also form a pyramid with the Sherbet Eater at the top. The story shows that a break in the chain is disastrous for the Giant Sherbet Eater.

The Giant Sherbet Eater: Once upon a time, there was a Giant Sherbet Eater. The Giant Sherbet Eater had a mouth like a long straw, so she was able to suck up sherbet when she was hungry. There was only one Giant Sherbet Eater, because there was never enough sherbet for more. It took five sherbet-makers to make all the sherbet she needed. It took twenty-five sugar growers to collect all the sugar that the sherbet-makers used. It took a hundred and twenty-five fields of sugar plants to make all the sugar they had to collect. It was a big operation, but they were all happy because they all had a job to do.

One day, one of the five sherbet-makers went down with sherbet-maker's sneezing fever. There's nothing worse than sherbet-maker's sneezing fever. One sneeze and great clouds of sherbet powder fill the air, so you sneeze for ever. Then another and another sherbet-maker went down with it. The Giant Sherbet Eater just couldn't get enough sherbet. She became thinner and thinner, and at last she died. The sherbet-makers that were left had no one to make sherbet for, and they died. The sugar-growers had no one to grow sugar for, and they died. All that was left were the fields of sugar plants. With no one to tend them, the sugar plants were pushed aside by grass and trees, so they died. Now there is nothing left to tell us that the sherbet people once lived here. You would never know that they had ever existed.

Talk: *Why did everyone die? Was it because the Giant Sherbet Eater became ill? Why didn't the hungry Giant Sherbet Eater just have a slice of bread and jam? How many sherbet-makers depended on the Giant Sherbet Eater? How many sugar-growers depended on them? How many fields of sugar plants depended on them? Is there a pattern to this? What is it? What do sugar plants depend on?* (You could build the food pyramid to make a visible representation using blocks. The first layer would be the fields of sugar plants (125), so would need 'lots' of blocks. Subsequent layers, in different colours, could be made with the exact numbers: 25, 5, 1.)

Step 2: What eats what?

This step helps the children construct food chains for a pond community. Focus your discussion on what eats what and build up some food chains on the chalkboard. Some parts of the food chains will be the same, so can be linked to make a food web (as in Figure 2.4). If the habitat you have introduced is a different one, simply adjust the words to suit that.

Talk: *What do frogs eat?* (Flies, moths, other insects.) *They must be hard to catch; what makes*

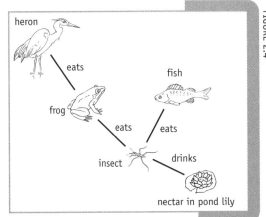

FIGURE 2.4

frogs good at catching insects? (They have a long, sticky tongue that flicks out and catches the insects.) *What do insects eat?* (Some eat leaves and leave holes in them. Some drink the nectar that flowers make.) *What kinds of leaves and flowers were in or near the pond?* (Weeds, rushes.) *What do these plants need to live?* (Sun, air, things in the soil.) *Does anything eat frogs?* (There's a bird called a heron that will eat frogs.) *What else was in the pond?* (Fish.) *What do fish eat?* (And so on.)

Step 3: Using ideas from 'The Giant Sherbet Eater' to help children grasp the relationships in the habitat

Here, you draw parallels with 'The Giant Sherbet Eater'. In particular, focus on the increasing numbers of individuals as you move down a food chain towards the plants. Then discuss what could happen if one link in the chain suffered a setback. (If the habitat you are introducing is different, adjust the words to suit it.)

Talk: *Do you remember the story of the Giant Sherbet Eater? Which pond animal is a bit like the Giant Sherbet Eater?* (The heron.) *What is a bit like the sugar plants?* (The pond plants.) *Were there lots of insects? What about frogs? Were there more frogs than insects? Why not? Would there be more herons than frogs? Why not? Do you remember what happened when the sherbet-makers became sick? What might happen if the insects all became sick and died? Why do you think that? What might happen if the Sun went out for weeks and weeks? Why do you think that?*

Step 4: The same pattern everywhere

This step is only relevant if you have already taught about another habitat. The aim is to draw out similarities and differences: although the living things are different, they depend on one another and each layer of life rests on one with greater numbers beneath. To illustrate this, compare food chains in a pond and a hedgerow:

Talk: *Think about when you watched the animals in the hedgerow. Were there lots of hedgehogs? No. That's a bit like which animal in the pond? What do hedgehogs eat?* (Worms and beetles.) *Were there more worms and beetles than hedgehogs? Think about the pond. What are like the hedgehog's worms and beetles? Are there any other things that are the same? What differences are there?*

More to talk about and do

Other habitats and threats to them

After looking at habitats that surround the children, you can introduce more remote ones, such as the rain forest, desert and tundra. Again, draw parallels between them and ones the children know well. The encroachment of people on these habitats often removes a fundamental level of the food web, namely plants, and this is a serious threat to the survival of everything above it. There are several books on this subject, particularly to do with the rain forests. You could have the children write about it from the viewpoint of one of the animals threatened.

Hands-on: leaf litter

Place a few handfuls of fresh leaf litter in a plastic aquarium. Ask the children to sort and classify what they find. (There will probably be a few small insects and insect-like animals among the leaves. Some leaves will also show signs of having been partly eaten.) Ask what other animals and plants, not in the aquarium, might be involved. *What eats what? How many of each one might there be?* (The children should wear appropriate hand protection, such as plastic or rubber gloves.)

Hands-on: soil

Place a handful of fresh, damp soil in a plastic aquarium. Have the children sort it and list what they find. They should wear hand protection, such as plastic or rubber gloves. Ask: *How do the tiny animals survive in the soil? What do they eat? What might eat them?*

Checking for understanding

Check on the children's understanding with questions and tasks, such as:

▶ *Ladybird grubs – the young of ladybirds – eat greenfly. Greenfly suck the sap from plants. Do you think there will be more greenfly than ladybirds or more ladybirds than greenfly? Why do you think that?*

▶ *You land on another world and see lots of living things you have never seen before. Sort them out into what you think might be a food chain. Explain why you did it like that.* (See Photocopiable Thinksheet 14 on page 73.)

▶ *Suppose you found an animal in another country that liked to live in pools of water. You know it eats insects and can catch them even better than a frog can. You bring it home and put it into the pond near where you live. What would probably happen? Why?*

> **Related topics**
> ▶ Animals (page 40)
> ▶ Green plants (page 51)
> ▶ Life (page 56).

Green plants

What are plants?

There are many different kinds of plant. Apart from the simplest plants, such as mosses, they all have a network that takes water from the roots to all parts of the plant. The veins you can see in leaves are a part of this network. Plants make what they need from soil-water and part of the air, using sunlight to make the substances combine. (Animals cannot do this.) In a flowering plant, this food-making activity takes place mainly in the leaves. Flowers help the plant reproduce. They attract insects, which pollinate the flowers. Parts of plants may move. For example, leaves and stems may turn to face the sun; flowers may open when the weather or time of day is right. The seeds that plants produce may be dispersed in various ways: the wind may blow them away, water may wash them to a new place, or they may stick to an animal's coat or be eaten and dropped somewhere else.

Understanding plants

Children tend to subdivide the plant world in a different way from scientists. For example, they may think in terms of: flowers, trees, bushes, grass and pot plants. Of course, these are all plants. The aim here is to widen the meaning of *plant* for children and clarify some of its important sub-groups.

Steps to understanding

Digging up wild plants is generally against the law, but you should be able to find what you want in the greengrocer's, among the weeds and flowering plants in a garden, on the school field or around the edges of the playground. The sequence of steps begins by comparing edible plants. (Photocopiable Thinksheet 15 on page 74 shows some examples, but you could use what you have to hand if you prefer.)

Age range and duration

Most children can follow these steps, though you should expect more complex responses from the older children. You would need up to 2 hours if you took all the steps in one go, but you will probably want a break after Step 3. This would be a good time to give the children their own hands-on activity.

Step 1: Same but different

In this step, you prepare the children for the later steps by having them compare and contrast two familiar plants. The plants are any that can be obtained from a greengrocer, such as a lettuce and a radish. Begin by showing the lettuce, then the radish. You will eventually need to cut the plants in half to show what is inside.

Talk: *I'm sure you all know what this is. It's a...? What about this? They look very different, don't they? Tell me one thing that's different. But look, there are some things that are the same. Can you tell me one? What about another?* (For example, parts that are green, parts that go under the ground, leaves.) *Watch, I'm going to cut them. Can you see anything else that is the same?* (You could continue by comparing these with a third plant of this kind, such as a cauliflower.)

Step 2: What plants have in common

In this step, you have the children examine a range of plants and look for things that they have in common. Photocopiable Thinksheet 15 on page 74 shows how to do this in a sequence that moves (anticlockwise) from soft, green plants to woody plants. This will help you to show that plants generally have:

▶ parts that are green (if you scrape the bark of a fresh woody plant, you should be able to reveal a green layer)
▶ roots below the ground
▶ supporting stems above ground
▶ leaves
▶ veins of some sort for carrying water (often visible if you hold a leaf up to the light)
▶ flowers at a certain time of the year.

Compare the pairs of plants on the sheet, moving around the loop until you compare the fir tree and the lettuce.

Talk: *Tell me what's the same about the radish and the onion. What about the onion and the grass?* (Continue through the sequence of plants, comparing them in pairs. Finally, complete the circle by comparing the lettuce and the fir tree. The leaves on a conifer are very narrow and needle-shaped. Photocopiable Thinksheet 15 on page 74 will help you work through the comparisons, but pictures are not really a substitute for the real thing.)

Step 3: Some differences between plants and two groups

Plants are extremely varied, so differences are easy to spot. Repeat the procedure used in Step 2, but have the children look for differences between the plants. Distinguish between two major groups of plants at this stage: woody-stemmed plants (many bushes and trees) and soft-stemmed plants (some house plants, edible plants and grasses).

Talk: *There are lots of plants, but they are all a bit different. Look, I'm going to make two groups of plants.* (Put all the woody plants into one group and the soft-stemmed plants into another.) *How are they different? These are woody plants. Why are they called woody plants? These are soft-stemmed plants. Why do you think they are called that?*

Step 4: Odds and ends of plants

Some plants may not seem to fit the pattern. Children find these interesting. This is the point where you can introduce one or two, such as a cactus or a Venus fly trap.

Talk: *Is this a plant? What makes you think that? Why does it have sharp spines?*

Step 5: Compare plants and animals
Take the opportunity to highlight a few differences between plants and animals.

Talk: *What can you do that a plant can't do? Is there anything the plant can do that you can't do? Is there anything about a plant and you that is the same?*

More to talk about and do
Some other characteristics of green plants to talk about
The topic of plants provides opportunities for discussion. For instance, if you show the children a cut log, they can talk about how a new ring is made each year. Have the children count the rings and find the log's age when it was cut down. You can also show the movement of water through a plant's stem by standing a stick of celery (with its leaves) in a vase of water coloured with a food dye (Figure 2.5). After the stem shows signs of colour, cut it across and pass the pieces around for the children to see the plant's 'veins'. Do not forget to tell the children never to taste plants or seeds as they may be poisonous.

FIGURE 2.5

Hands-on: variety where everything seemed the same
Children may think that grasses are all the same. Have them look for different grasses along the edges of the school field or school playground. How many can they find? How are they different? How are they the same? Children may think of tree leaves in much the same way. A collection of leaves can show their variety. Similarly, bark rubbings can highlight differences in bark patterns. Children can examine and note the differences.

Hands-on: plants that like the light
If the children grow cress from seed, they can place the pots of cress so that light comes only from one side. The cress will quickly bend towards the light as it grows.

Checking for understanding
Check on the children's understanding with questions and tasks, such as:
▶ *Are you a plant? How do you know you are not a plant?*
▶ Show a piece of tree bark. Ask: *Did this once belong to a plant? Was it a woody plant or a soft plant? What could the rest of it look like? Why do you think that?*
▶ *What would happen to a plant if you took all its leaves away? Why?*

> **Related topics**
> ▶ Life (page 56)
> ▶ Plant food (page 61).

Hearing

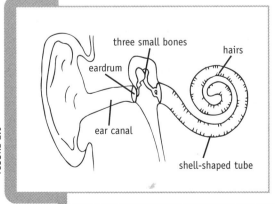

FIGURE 2.6

three small bones
hairs
eardrum
ear canal
shell-shaped tube

How do we hear?
The ear (see Figure 2.6) comprises a flap that we can see, a tube into the head, and an eardrum at the end of the tube that covers a cavity containing three small bones and a coiled tube lined with hairs. (There are also parts to do with balance, but these are ignored here.) The flap helps to catch sound vibrations in the air. These pass down the tube and make the thin skin of the eardrum vibrate. The vibrations are passed on through the small bones to the coiled tube. The hairs

in this tube can vibrate, but some hairs respond better to high notes and others respond better to low notes. Nerves at the roots of the hairs let the brain know which hairs are vibrating, a sensation we know as sound.

Understanding how we hear

Children may think that the ear comprises only an outer flap and a hole into the head. They think that sounds pass into the head via the hole and are somehow detected directly. There is a lot of science and mechanics involved in the workings of the ear, and learning how it works is a worthwhile exercise.

Steps to understanding

The steps take the children through the function of each part of the ear in turn. While you can take these steps in a continuous sequence, each can be treated as a sub-topic. Learning about hearing teaches children about themselves and one of their senses, but it also develops the children's knowledge of sound.

Age range and duration

The topic is better suited to older children. Putting aside time for other activities, you will need at least half an hour for each step.

Step 1: The outer ear

The first step is to start with the visible bit: the sound catcher. You will need some thin card and safe scissors for the children to make large ears (two A4 pieces of card per child). During the following talk, have the children use cupped hands to catch more sound, then have them make bigger ears from the card and test them.

> **Talk:** *What are these?* (Indicate the visible ears.) *What do they do? Suppose they were bigger? Would that make a difference? Let's try it – cup your hands like this, place them behind your ears and listen to me talk. Does it sound different? Why is that? Suppose we made even bigger ears. What difference would that make?* (Have the children make large ears from card and test them as they did their cupped hands.) *So what do you think our ear flaps are for?*

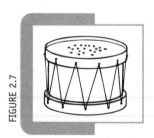

FIGURE 2.7

Step 2: The eardrum

This step has to do with the action of the eardrum. You need a drum or a large plastic basin with a piece from a plastic bag stretched taut over it, so that it behaves like a small drum. Sprinkle a few grains of sand on to the drum 'skin' (see Figure 2.7). Make a loud noise nearby (clap hands). The grains of sand should jump a little in response.

> **Talk:** *Where do your sound catchers send the sounds? The end of the tube in your head has a piece of skin over it to make it like a drum. Can you guess what it is called? What do you think it does? When I talk, what does it make the air do? What do you think shaking/vibrating air does to the skin on the ear drum?* (Have the children examine the real drum to help their speculations. Sprinkle a few grains of sand on the drum skin. Clap your hands close to the drum top and draw the children's attention to the way the sand jumps slightly in response.) *So sounds will make the eardrum shake/vibrate. What will that do to these little bones?* (Indicate the bones on a picture of the ear.)

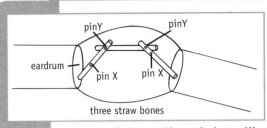

FIGURE 2.8

eardrum

pinY   pinY

pin X   pin X

three straw bones

Step 3: Magnifying vibrations in the ear

The three small bones behave like levers and magnify the tiny vibrations of the eardrum. The way levers can magnify a small movement to make a bigger one can be shown using lollipop sticks, straws or strip wood. Figure 2.8 shows three straws connected with pins to form a linkage. These behave like our ear bones and magnify the small movements of the eardrum. (Photocopiable Thinksheet 16 on page 75 shows how to arrange the straws so that the children can try it for themselves.)

Talk: *Do you think the eardrum moves very much? It probably only moves backwards and forwards a tiny amount. I'll bet you'd need a magnifier to see it. These little bones make the movement bigger. How can they do that? Watch this straw. When I wiggle this end just a little bit, how much does the other end move? (Indicate the other end.) Why does it move more at that end? Faint sounds hardly move the eardrum at all, but the bones make the tiny movements bigger at the other end.*

Step 4: Getting the message to the brain

The final step is to help the children grasp how the vibrations make the hairs in the tube move, a movement that is detected by the nerves at the hair roots. You need two tuning forks that make the same pitched note. The children will have to be silent. Ask a child to press the heel of one fork to a tabletop. As it is not vibrating, there should be no sound. Make the other fork vibrate by hitting it on a book and press its heel to the tabletop, near the first fork. After two or three seconds, stop your fork by holding the tines. Have the children listen carefully to the other fork. It should be vibrating gently and making a faint sound (Figure 2.9).

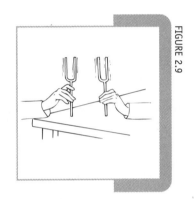

FIGURE 2.9

Talk: *See how the shaking of this tuning fork makes the other one shake, too? It's a bit like that in your ears. This tube (indicating the picture) has tiny hairs in it. When the bones send vibrations into the tube, it makes hairs shake. At the root of each hair is a nerve. You can feel nerves when you pull a hair on your arm. They send a message to your brain that tells it someone is tugging on the hair. In your ear, the nerve sends a message to your brain and tells it that the hair is shaking. Your brain knows that this must mean a sound made that happen.*

FIGURE 2.10

More to talk about and do

Deafness

Talk about some causes of deafness. For instance, the eardrum may be perforated or the small bones may become stuck together so they cannot pass on vibrations. Of course, a reduction in hearing is often the result of an excess of ear wax that blocks the outer tube. This can be flushed out by a doctor.

Hands-on: make and test an ear trumpet

The children may extend the activity on making model ears to make a simple, conical ear trumpet (Figure 2.10). In Victorian times, this was a device used by people who were hard of hearing. Animals can often turn their ears to catch sounds. Some people have a vestige of this ability. (But not all large ears are only to catch sound. Elephant ears also seem to serve as radiators that help them keep cool.)

Checking for understanding
Check on the children's understanding with questions and tasks, such as:

Related topics
Sound (page 141).

- *I clap my hands like this and the sound spreads out until it reaches your ears. Tell me where it goes next and what happens. And after that?* (and so on)
- *Very loud sounds can injure your ears so you become deaf. Why is that?*
- *How do ear defenders help to protect you from ear damage? If we were to make our own, how would we do it?*

Life

What do 'living' and 'non-living' mean?

There are two major types of things in the world: living and non-living. The non-living may be further divided into once-lived and never-lived. Living things have the ability to breathe, feed, grow, move, excrete and reproduce. They can also sense their surroundings. Generally, these abilities are signs of life. They make sense to children and help them divide the world into these two important groups. At the microscopic level, however, classification is not always simple, and scientists continue to explore and debate the characteristics of life.

Understanding the concept of life

Children generally know that a stone, for instance, lacks whatever it takes to be alive. As far as they are concerned, it lies there and does nothing and things just happen to it. A dog, on the other hand, does things itself. If you poke it, it responds, just as you would. Animals tend to be easy to classify as living. In between the stone and the dog, however, it can be a less certain world. Young children may hesitate to say that a plant is alive. Even older children can be uncertain about how to classify a fungus on a dead tree, a lichen on a wall, a patch of mould on a brick, a flame, and a once-living object such as a dead leaf. You will have to help children divide the world into living and non-living. They must learn not to be confused by something having once been alive, or by seeing it grow on something that is dead.

For ourselves, we must also distinguish between the child's play thinking and their real beliefs. For instance, a child who acts as if a teddy bear is alive often knows that Teddy is not alive. A child may even place Teddy in the living group, but even this does not necessarily mean that the child really believes Teddy is alive. It can be quite difficult for children to be detached about items that have an emotional significance for them.

Steps to understanding

The first three steps provide the foundation (living and non-living), and the fourth and fifth steps take it further (once-living and puzzling cases).

Age range and duration

This topic is suitable for all ages. The foundations (Steps 1 to 3) are generally laid with younger children. The steps should not be rushed. In particular, allow up to an hour for the first one if you are to provide time for observation, discussion and some form of recording. Allow another hour for Steps 2 and 3, and up to an hour for the last two steps.

Step 1: Some characteristics of living things

Have ready a small collection of living things that show a range of features. For example, you might show a guinea pig, a goldfish, a snail, a common flowering plant and, perhaps, a plant that can move, such as a sensitive plant (mimosa) or a Venus flytrap from a garden centre. You can, of course, use whatever living things are available. Reveal the thing that exhibits the most obvious characteristics first (probably the guinea pig or fish) and progress through the collection to the least obvious (probably the flowering plant).

Talk: *What is it? Is it alive? Why do you think it is alive? What does it do that makes us think it's alive?* (Try to elicit the characteristics of life: moves about by itself, eats, excretes, grows up, breathes, makes young ones that grow up like itself. The most difficult characteristic to elicit is probably sensitivity.) *Does it know when you touch it? How do we know it does? Do you think it knows when it is light or dark? Do you think it knows when the room is cold?* (Look for characteristics of life in the rest of the collection.) *Does the goldfish breathe? It does but not as we do. There is air in the water and it breathes that. Does the snail move? How do we know?* If you have a sensitive plant or a Venus flytrap: *Can a plant move by itself? Watch. I'm going to touch the leaf with a piece of paper. See it close? Why does it do that?* Otherwise: *Can a plant move by itself? Have you ever seen how plants bend towards the sunlight? Let's leave this one and see if it moves towards the sunlight.*

Step 2: Some characteristics of non-living things

Have ready a collection of non-living things that represent a range of features (such as a stone, a cup, a beaker of water, a metal spoon, a brick, a marble, some modelling clay). Reveal them one by one and discuss whether or not they shows signs of life.

Talk: What's this? Is it alive? Why do you think it is not alive? Does it move about by itself? Does it eat things? Does it poop? Did it grow up? Does it breathe? Does it make young ones to grow up like itself?

Step 3: Distinguishing between living and non-living things

Show a small, mixed collection (such as an insect, a piece of chalk, a rose, a badge). Have the children classify them and justify their classification.

Talk: *So you think that is alive? Tell me why you think that.*

Step 4: Once-living things

Introduce a collection of once-living items (such as a dead twig, a painted piece of wood, a cork mat, a piece of paper). By discussion, establish that the dead twig no longer exhibits the characteristics of life, so should not be included with living things. Sometimes, once-living things can have been changed so much it is hard to tell that they were once living. Introduce the painted piece of wood, the cork and the paper. Explore the origins of each with the children.

Talk: *What is it? Where did it come from? Is it alive or dead? Which group should we put it in, living or non-living?*

Step 5: Living or non-living?

Show some less clear-cut items (such as a potato, a mushroom from the supermarket, a stone with lichen on it). Discuss what they are and describe how they grow and show signs of life.

Talk: *What is it? Is it living or non-living? What should we look for? What evidence have we got? So do you think it is alive?*

More to talk about and do

Some ambiguous cases to talk about

There will still be things that are a puzzle. First, there are things that do not show the characteristics of life in an obvious way and that it is difficult, unsafe or unwise to introduce to the classroom. Germs are an example. Then there are things that we know are not alive but that appear to show characteristics of life, such as fire. Fire moves and 'eats' up things in the process, it consumes oxygen and can grow, it leaves ash behind and can generate other fires from its sparks. However, it is not sensitive to its environment. Crystals also grow, but do not show other signs of life. Use Photocopiable Thinksheet 17 on page 76 to provoke discussion of the characteristics of life.

Hands-on: expanding experience of the living and non-living world

Hands-on activities were included in the steps above, and should continue whenever something new turns up or a new environment is explored.

Related topics
▶ Animals (page 40)
▶ Green plants (page 51)
▶ Microbes (page 58).

Checking for understanding

Check children's understanding with questions and tasks, such as:
▶ *Look at this toy car: it moves, makes a noise and consumes electricity from batteries. Is it alive? Why do you think it is not alive?*
▶ *Convince me that you are alive and not just like a table.*
▶ *Is water in a waterfall alive? Why do you think it is not alive?*

Microbes

What is a microbe?

A microbe or micro-organism is a minute living thing. It is generally too small to be seen by the unaided eye. A microscope extends the ability of our eyes so that we can see some of this normally invisible world. Some microbes are beneficial, such as the yeast that makes bread rise, microbes that turn milk into cheese and yoghurt, and microbes that break down dead materials in soil and compost heaps to produce materials that plants need to grow. There are even microbes that help us digest food. Others are a nuisance, such as those that turn milk sour, bread mouldy and eggs bad. Some do us harm, as when they rot teeth or give us spots. Microbes are everywhere: in the air, in the soil, on us and in us. Like all living things, microbes need moisture, food and warmth. Take any of these away and they cannot thrive. A refrigerator makes food last longer because it denies microbes warmth. Drying food denies them moisture. Heat kills microbes, as it does when we cook food thoroughly. Microbes can also be killed by certain chemicals, such as those used to clean the lavatory bowl. Thorough scrubbing with soap will also remove many of them, as when a surgeon scrubs up before surgery.

Understanding microbes

The first problem for children when trying to understand microbes is that this is an invisible world. The second is that microbes are very different from the living things they have met before. Children may not see microbes as a part of the normal living world, and having the same characteristics of life as bigger living things. The third problem is that children tend to hear of microbes in connection with illness, so microbes may be thought to be universally bad. Many aspects of the topic are not open to practical investigation, as you must not increase children's exposure to potentially harmful microbes. The aim is to help children appreciate that there is a microscopic world of living things – some beneficial, some harmless and some harmful. They should also understand how to prevent infections.

Steps to understanding

The first step helps the child to appreciate the existence of the microscopic world. Subsequent steps look at beneficial and harmful microbes and give the children an understanding of hygienic practices.

Age range and duration

This topic is generally dealt with in classes of older children. Step 1 can take half an hour or more, depending on how many things you give the children to examine. The remaining steps, if done in a sequence and with some written work, need at least an hour. The supplementary activities will obviously need additional time.

Step 1: Making the invisible world visible

You need a magnifier and, if possible, a simple microscope. Have a variety of materials for the children to examine, such as salt and a spoonful of soil. Show them how to use the magnifier and let them see and draw the rich world that is just out of sight. If you have a microscope, you can take this further.

Talk: (Have the children examine the salt.) *What do you see? Did that surprise you? Why?* (Have them examine the soil.) *What do you see? Is there anything alive? How do you know it's alive? If you could look even closer, what do you think you would find?* You might introduce and discuss the verse: *Big fleas have little fleas upon their backs to bite 'em. Little fleas have smaller fleas, and so ad infinitum.* You will probably need to explain that 'and so ad infinitum' means 'and so on, for ever'.

Step 2: Beneficial microbes

Have available: bread yeast and a slice of bread, yoghurt, gut bacteria supplement (for example, Yakult® or Actimel®), a piece of veined cheese. Yeast comprises millions of microbial spores that, in the right conditions, make a gas. The gas bubbles make the bread rise and leave lots of tiny holes in it. Microbes turn milk into yoghurt and are still in it when you eat it. Microbes help to break down food inside us. Some say that supplementing the microbes in our guts improves digestion. Microbes make the veins in some cheeses and most of the smell. Many people like the taste of 'blue' cheeses.

Talk: Begin with the cheese. *What's this? How did the coloured marks get there? Microbes were put into the cheese deliberately. When they grow, they make these coloured marks – and most of the smell. Some people like the taste. Look at this.* (Show the yeast.) *This is a lump made up of millions of microbes. Do you know what they are used for?* (Show the slice of bread.) *They are used to put the air holes in bread.* (Set some yeast to ferment and produce frothy gas bubbles in sugary, lukewarm water, as in Figure 2.11. Describe what the yeast does in bread dough.) *These are useful microbes. There are also useful microbes in the soil. They break up dead things so that the plants have something to help them grow.*

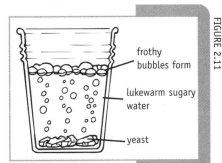

frothy bubbles form

lukewarm sugary water

yeast

FIGURE 2.11

Step 3: Harmful microbes

Having made the point that there are beneficial microbes, you can now discuss less helpful microbes. Have the children recall foodstuffs made unusable by microbe action, such as sour milk, mouldy bread and bad eggs. Talk about the action of microbes in causing tooth decay. Move on to illness and disease-causing microbes, such as those that cause sore throats, boils, infections in cuts and grazes, measles and typhoid fever.

Talk: *What happens to moist bread if you leave it where it is warm? Why does it do that? What about a bottle of milk? How is sour milk different to fresh milk? What does it remind you of? (Yoghurt.) What makes it like that? Have you ever smelled bad eggs? Do you remember how the cheese smelled? Why do eggs make that awful smell? We have to be very careful with food that goes off. You can't eat it – it might make you very ill. What about us? Can bad microbes get into us? What do they do? How do they make you feel?*

Step 4: Preventing microbes doing what we don't want

There are three parts in this step (supported by simple visual aids, if available):
▶ removing microbes from our hands (using a dish, soap, water and a nail brush)
▶ killing microbes with heat or chemicals (using a sterilising spray for kitchen surfaces)
▶ preventing microbes multiplying by denying them water, food or warmth (have ready a dry slice of toast, a moist slice of bread, dried peas).
Take each in turn and discuss it.

Talk: *Why should we wash our hands before eating? What are we trying to remove? Look, I'm scrubbing my fingernails with a nail brush. Why is that a good thing? Have you ever seen doctors on the TV scrub their hands before they do an operation? Do you know why they do that? (Show the spray.) What does the can say this is? Bacteria are microbes and some can be bad for you. Disinfectants kill bacteria, but some are so strong that they can damage your skin or your eyes. They are used in toilets and drains. Microbes are living things, just like you and me. They like water, food and warmth. Why does a fridge make food last longer? What about these peas? Will they last a long time? Why? Will this piece of toast last longer than the slice of bread? Why? Why should we keep surfaces wiped clean? If there is nothing for the microbes to live on, then they can't multiply. What about flies and other bugs? Why do we not want them in our houses?*

More to talk about and do

If I were the size of a microbe

Have the children imagine that someone has shrunk them to the size of a microbe. What would it be like? Suppose they were on a slice of bread and were swallowed by a normal-sized person. What would their adventure be like? See Photocopiable Thinksheet 18 on page 77 for another perspective.

Hands-on: bread-making

First, you could have the children investigate yeast action. What makes it more active? Would it work better in the refrigerator? Would it work better near a radiator, or in the sun? After this, you could have the children make bread dough. They could let it 'prove' (make it rise by putting it in a warm place). If you go on to bake the bread, you should do the baking and deal with the oven yourself for the children's safety. The heat of the baking kills the yeast.

Hands-on: who has had which microbes inside them?

Have the children collect data about the infectious illnesses they have had and present their data using their ICT skills.

Checking for understanding

Check on the children's understanding with questions and tasks, such as:
▶ *Why are living things that are too small to see called microbes or micro-organisms?*

▶ *Microbes help us turn unwanted parts of plants into compost for the garden. The picture shows how this is done (see Photocopiable Thinksheet 18 on page 77). How do the pipes with holes in them help?* (Microbes need air and these pipes let air in.) *The gardener has to sprinkle water on the garden waste from time to time. Why does this help?* (Microbes need water and this provides it.) *Which part of the year do you think is best for compost-making?* (Summer.) *Why?* (Microbes need warmth and it is warmer in summer.)

▶ *People say, 'Coughs and sneezes spread diseases'. Why do coughs and sneezes spread diseases? If you had a cold, what could you do so that other people do not catch it from you?*

Related topics
▶ Life (page 56)
▶ Changes (page 80)
▶ Digestion (page 45).

Plant food

What is food-making in green plants?

Unlike animals, green plants do not have to look for ready-made food. Most of them make what they need from the basic ingredients. This happens in the green parts of the plant, such as the leaves. There are small holes in the leaves that let air in. Water comes up to the leaves from the roots. Sunlight energy helps carbon dioxide and water join together to make sugars. These sugars are the plant's food. The plant uses the sugars for life processes, such as growth. Plants such as potatoes and turnips change these sugars into starch, which they store in their roots. Animals often take advantage of this ready-made, pre-packed food supply.

The leaf is often described as a chemical factory that takes in raw materials and makes them into sugars. However, if you simply mix air and water, even on a sunny day, you will not end up with plant sugars. The leaf also contains chlorophyll which can bring the raw materials together in the right way. Making plant sugars in this way is called *photosynthesis*. Plants also take in other materials, especially those that dissolve in the soil water. They use these to change the sugars into new plant tissue. Fertilisers make plants grow better because they supply more of these materials.

Understanding food-making in green plants

Children tend to think that plants do not make their own food but take it in through their roots, ready-made. This idea is supported by labels on fertilisers that say 'plant food'. The aim here is to help the children understand that green plants make their own food.

Steps to understanding

This is not a topic that lends itself well to a 'watch it and learn' approach, because what is happening inside the leaf cannot be seen. These steps introduce the substances involved in a plant's food-making activities, and describe what happens using the factory-in-a-leaf metaphor.

Age range and duration

This is a topic that is better suited to older children. The steps need about an hour to complete if taken in one sitting, but it is probably better to intersperse them with some written or similar activity.

Step 1: When animals need food

Have the children reflect on what we and other animals do when we need food. In our case, we buy it ready-made in shops. All cooking does is make it more tasty or easier to eat or digest. Some animals eat other animals and some animals eat plants. But what do plants do?

Talk: *What do you do when you need some food? What about a different animal, like a fox? What does a cow do when it needs food? Animal food is all ready-made. I know we sometimes have to cook it, but we could eat everything raw if we really had to. We don't have to go around looking for all the things that an apple is made from and put them together to make an apple. We just find an apple and eat it. But what do plants do? We don't see them in supermarkets and we don't see them taking bites out of cows or taking bites out of each other. Where do they get their food?*

Step 2: When plants need food

You need a wooden peg, a few scraps of fabric and two elastic bands. Ask the children what people do if they cannot get what they want ready-made. Tell them about children long ago who could not afford a doll. They had to make their own. Quickly show them how (Figure 2.12). The ingredients (peg, fabric scraps and elastic bands) become a doll. Plants have to collect the ingredients they need and make them into their food themselves.

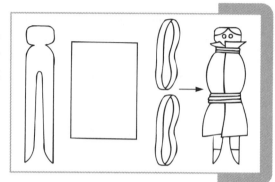

FIGURE 2.12

Talk: *When you want something but cannot get it ready-made, what do you have to do? A long time ago, only rich children could afford to buy dolls. What do you think poor children did? They made their own. Watch, I'll show you how they did it. They start off with the bits you need – the ingredients – and make them into a doll. Plants have to do that when they make food. They have to collect the bits they need and make them into plant food.*

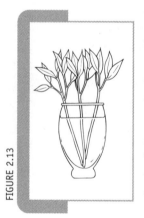

FIGURE 2.13

Step 3: The plant's factories

You need some leafy plant stems in a transparent plastic container (Figure 2.13). Use this to introduce the leaf as the place where the action is – the plant's food factory. Use a car factory as a simple analogy: components go in, special tools fit them together, and cars come out. The raw ingredients for a plant are air and water. Draw attention to the air that surrounds the plants in the container, and show that plants takes up water. (Place the container in a sunny place and have the children mark the water level. After a while, they will see that it has fallen as the stems take up water.) These ingredients are put together to make plant sugars with the help of sunlight. The special tool that does the making is *chlorophyll*.

Talk: *Here's how plants do it. What are these? (Leaves.) Leaves are where plants make their food. They are food factories for the plant. Think about a car factory powered by electricity. What are the bits a car factory needs to make a car? These bits go into the factory and special tools fit them together to make cars. It's a bit like that in a leaf factory. Leaf factories are powered by sunlight. What is it that is all around the leaves? (Air.) There are tiny holes in the leaves that let the air in. What's this in the vase? (Water.) See how it has gone down? The water has gone up the stems into the leaves. The special tool in a leaf is a chemical called chlorophyll. With the help of sunlight, it joins water, things in the water and some of the air together to make what the plant needs to grow.*

Step 4: What photosynthesis means

This step explains the meaning of the word *photosynthesis*. Begin by reminding children of simpler words, like 'welding'.

Talk: *Do you know what 'welding' means? Welding is when pieces of metal are joined together using heat. What leaves do is join things together using sunlight. Scientists call it photosynthesis. It's really two words:* photo *and* synthesis. *'Photo' means 'light'. Do you know any other words with 'photo' in? What do you think 'synthesis' means? It means 'joining together'. So what does 'photosynthesis' mean?*

More to talk about and do

The food factory in winter

Talk about deciduous and evergreen plants. Deciduous trees lose their leaves in winter. This means that they do not have food factories during the coldest, darkest part of the year. They are dormant in winter. Most green plants, even those that keep their leaves, are less active in winter.

Hands-on: what affects how much water plants take in?

As the children observe the plant taking up water in the container, ask them when it takes up the most water. Is it when the plant is in the sun or when it is in the shade? Ask the children what they think will happen, and why they think that. Encourage them to test their ideas.

Checking for understanding

Check on the children's understanding with questions and tasks, such as:

▶ *Some green plants lose their leaves in winter. Can they still make food for themselves? Why not?*

▶ *In trees, water comes up from the roots and rises through the inner bark to the branches. Sometimes beavers chew the bark off trees all the way around the trunk. What do you think happens to the tree? Why?*

▶ *If all the plants in the world died out, what would happen to the animals? Why? If all the animals died out, what would happen to the plants? Why do you think that?*

> **Related topics**
> ▶ Chemical changes (page 82)
> ▶ Feeding relationships (page 48)
> ▶ Digestion (page 45).

Seeing

What is seeing?

We sense light with our eyes. Light from the scene enters our eyes and hits the back of the eyeball. The back of the eyeball has a lining (the *retina*) that makes tiny electrical currents when light falls on it. These electrical currents go along the *optic nerve* to the brain, which deals with the information. This is what we call 'seeing', and it is one of the ways we know about the world around us.

Understanding seeing

Children may think that their eyes emit light and this is what enables them to see things. This may be reinforced by the word 'look'. When we *look at* something, we direct our gaze at it. To a child, it may sound as though something is emitted by the eye at the object. In addition, the eye is a complex organ, and learning about its parts can obscure the more fundamental aspects. The aim here is to help the children grasp that the eye is a receiver of light, and this receiver helps us to know what is out there.

Steps to understanding

The sequence of steps is intended to reveal to you how a child may think about seeing.

It goes on to help the children understand that seeing is due to light entering the eye, not coming from it. The feeling that an eye is a kind of transmitter can be persistent. It helps if you revisit the topic and include some extension work.

Age range and duration

The steps are suited to intermediate and older children, and may take about one and a half hours to complete. You may prefer to take Step 4 (half an hour) on a different occasion and use it to remind the children of the earlier steps.

Step 1: How do your eyes work?

The first step allows you to explore the children's existing knowledge about seeing. You need a toy, initially kept out of sight. Have the children close and cover their eyes. Your conversation is intended to help the children express their ideas about how they think their eyes work.

Talk: *Close your eyes and cover them with your hands. Can you see anything? Keep your eyes closed. I'm holding something up. Do you know what is it? Take your hands away and open your eyes. What is it? How did your eyes help you? How do your eyes see things? What happens when you look at something?*

Step 2: Do eyes really send out something so that we can see?

The eyes receive light from things. Even children who give the 'correct' answer may know what you want them to say but not be fully convinced by it. Many could benefit by being provided with evidence. You need some boxes (for example, shoe boxes) containing a small object, such as a toy. The lids should be sealed. Make a small viewing hole at one end of each box (Figure 2.14). It is difficult to make out what is in the box when looking through the hole. This means that your eyes are not shining light into the box. If they were, you would only need to point them through the hole to see what is in the box.

FIGURE 2.14

Talk: *Why can you not see when you have a blindfold on? You think it's because your eyes cannot shine out when they are covered? Tell me how you see something in that corner. So you just look at it and your eyes sort of shine on it? What about this box? There's something inside. The lid won't come off but there's a small hole in the end. Could you look through there? Would that mean you could see inside? Have a try. What's inside the box? Oh, you can't see. Why not? Could your eyes 'shine' into the box? I wonder if your eyes really shine on things. What about when you go to bed and cover your head up? Can you see? You've got your eyes with you, so why isn't it as bright as day? Maybe eyes don't shine out after all.*

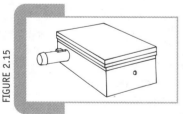

FIGURE 2.15

Step 3: Offering an alternative

Suggesting to the children that some of their ideas about seeing may be unsound is a start, but a feasible alternative is needed. You will need a shoebox with a torch inserted, as in Figure 2.15. This arrangement allows you to provide or withhold light in the box.

Talk: *Look at this box. It's got a torch fitted to it. The torch is off at the moment. Get your eyes ready. Put one eye next to the hole. Can you see anything yet? I'm switching the torch on... now! Can you see anything? What can you see? Why can you see it? What is helping you to see it? So light coming from the torch and shining on to things lets you see them. How does that help you see? Light doesn't come out* *of your eyes. Instead, light comes from something else and bounces off things into your eyes. That's how you see. How can we see in the classroom? There's no torch in the classroom, so how can we see in here? Where is the light coming from? Where does it go? Could some of it get into your eyes? If you stop it getting into your eyes, will you see anything?*

Step 4: My eyes are not like a pair of torches
This step obliges the child to differentiate between their eyes (receivers or detectors of light) and a torch (an emitter of light). You will need two battery-operated torches (one will do but two are better, as that is the same as the number of eyes we have). Hold both torches side by side and switch them on.

Talk: *Look at these torches. I've switched them on. Tell me how they are different to your eyes. How many ways can you think of?*

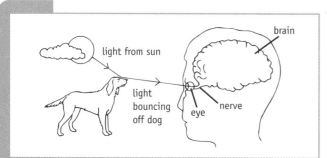

FIGURE 2.16

light from sun

light bouncing off dog

eye

nerve

brain

More to talk about and do
The structure of the eye
The eye is complex, but you can simplify its structure so that its basics can be understood. This will reinforce the steps above. In Figure 2.16, light bounces off the dog and heads towards your eyes. It goes through the black centre of your eye and hits the back. When the light hits the special cells lining the back of the eye, tiny amounts of electricity are produced. The nerve behaves like a wire. An impulse passes up the nerve to the brain, where it is processed so that we know the shape and colour of the dog in front of us.

This explanation can be taken a little further. The *iris* is the coloured ring around the black circle. When the light is too bright, the iris makes the black circle smaller so that less light gets in. In the dark, it makes the black circle bigger to let more light in (Figure 2.17).

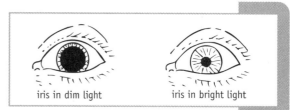

FIGURE 2.17

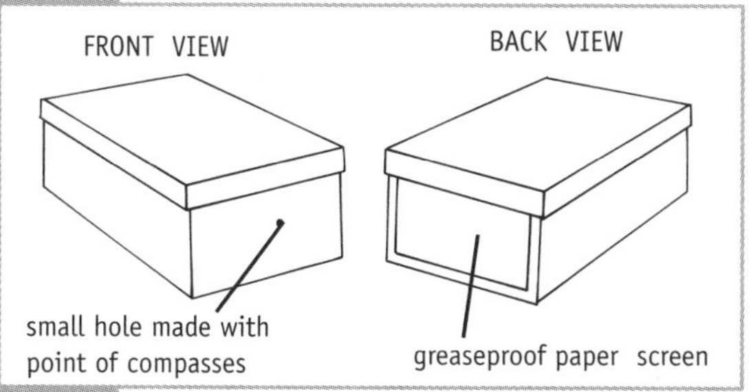

iris in dim light

iris in bright light

FRONT VIEW

BACK VIEW

small hole made with point of compasses

greaseproof paper screen

FIGURE 2.18

Hands-on: making a working model eye
The children can make a model eye using a shoe box. Have them replace one end with greaseproof paper. This will be like the back of the eye. Pierce the opposite end with the point of your compasses to make a small hole for the children. The children should then point the hole at a window. A picture of the window will appear on the screen (Figure 2.18). You should take the opportunity to point to the fact that light travels into the model eye from the window, and not out from it to the window. (The image of the window on the greaseproof paper will be upside-down. It is the same in the eye, but the brain can deal with that.)

Checking for understanding
Check on the children's understanding with questions and tasks, such as:
▶ *If you close your eyes, walk into a dark room and then open your eyes, will you be able to see? Why not?*
▶ *If our eyes actually sent out light, what difference would that make to our lives? Think about riding your bicycle in the dark.*

▶ *Young Johnny thinks that we can see because light shines out of our eyes on to the things in front of us. What would you do to show him he is wrong?*

Related topics
▶ Light sources (page 131)
▶ Hearing (page 53).

Skeleton

What is the skeleton and what is it for?

The skeleton in the human body comprises some 200 bones. Together, these make a frame that supports the body, protects its organs and provides anchor points for muscles. Major parts of the skeleton are the skull that protects the brain, the rib cage that helps us breathe and protects the chest organs, the leg and arm bones, and a backbone that supports the head and has places for attaching the pelvis and rib cage. Flexibility is achieved by moveable joints that connect the bones. The overall form of the human body is due to its skeleton. If the skeleton had a different form, we would look different.

Understanding the skeleton

Children often know a little about bones, but are not generally aware of what they do. The aim here is to help them understand these aspects of the skeleton.

Steps to understanding

Pictures and models generally show the complexity of the human skeleton, rather than its underlying simplicity. The first three steps explain the way the skeleton gives us shape, provides protection for our internal organs and enables us to move. The fourth step then simplifies the skeleton into a small number of units and reveals their properties by drawing parallels with familiar objects.

Age range and duration

To work through all the steps, you would need to set aside two hours or more; but this is not necessarily the best approach. Instead, you may wish to be selective and do Steps 1 to 3 in one sitting (about an hour, ignoring written and other activities you are likely to provide). Step 4 could be taken later (allowing an hour). If you feel the children would find Steps 1 and 2 self-evident, they may be omitted.

FIGURE 2.19

Step 1: What would we be like without a skeleton?

Introduce Mr Blobby, a very large plastic bag with eyes, nose and mouth marked on it (see Figure 2.19). Give Mr Blobby some body organs, such as a heart, lungs, stomach (made from small inflated bags or balloons) and intestines (thick string). With these organs inside Mr Blobby, dump him on the table so that he slowly subsides into a shapeless pile. Talk about why he has no fixed shape. (For safety, remove the plastic bags when you finish with them.)

Talk: *Oh dear, look at Mr Blobby; he just can't seem to stand up. Whatever I do with him, he just flops down. Why can't he stand up? Why does he not have a shape? What could we do to give him a shape? What do we have inside us that gives us a shape?*

FIGURE 2.20

Step 2: What difference does a skeleton make?

Give Mr Blobby a skeleton. Make a large, rectangular frame from strip wood to suit the size of the bag (see Figure 2.20). Talk about how this gives Mr Blobby a fixed shape.

Talk: *Let's give him a skeleton. Look at the one I've made for him. Does it work? Can he stand up? Why does he not look like us when we stand up? What would his skeleton have to be like to make him look like us? Does his skeleton protect his heart and lungs and the other things inside him? What could I do to his skeleton to protect his heart and lungs?*

Step 3: A model of a skeleton

Present a model skeleton made from a small box (as the skull) fixed on top of a larger box (the rib cage) and with cardboard tubes as the legs and arms, glued into place (Figure 2.21). The point is that this skeleton has many of the features of our skeleton, but it has no joints and so cannot move. This provides a way to introduce the concept of skeletal joints.

FIGURE 2.21

Talk: *How is this like a skeleton? Which bits are which? What's wrong with this skeleton? What can our skeletons do that it cannot do? How do our skeletons let us move? What can we do with our heads? How are we able to do that? What about our mouths? How can we open our mouths?*

Step 4a: The skull

The skull is rather like a builder's hard hat. Have a hard hat or child's cycle helmet to hand. Relate wearing a hard hat to having a skull to protect the brain. (Photocopiable Thinksheet 19 on page 78 shows the skull.)

Talk: *Why does a builder wear a hard hat? Are there any other hats like this? (Crash helmets, cyclists' helmets, riding hats, army helmets.) What's just under the skin of your head? What does it look like? What does it remind you of? What do you think it's for? How is it like a hard hat? How is it different from a hard hat? What does it have to do that a hard hat does not have to do? (For example, provide places for the eyes, nose and mouth.)*

Step 4b: The ribs

The ribs make a shape rather like a bird cage (or some similar item). Have such an item to hand (for example, a bird or animal cage, a letter tray, a hanging basket made from wire mesh). Show that a cage has strength and relate that to the rib cage. (Photocopiable Thinksheet 19 shows the rib cage.)

Talk: *See how thin the cage bars are. Try pressing on the cage. Is it strong? Does it keep its shape? Would a bird be safe inside it? Would it keep a cat out? Look at the ribs in the skeleton. Feel your own ribs. Do you know what is inside your ribs? Are your heart and lungs important? How do your ribs protect them?*

Step 4c: The backbone

The backbone is rather like a broom handle. Have a broom head, without its handle, available. Relate the function of the broom handle (as a support and lever) to the function of the backbone. (Photocopiable Thinksheet 19 shows the backbone.)

Talk: (Show the broom head.) *What's missing? What kind of handle do we need; should it be a thin, bendy one? So one that didn't bend would be better. What if we only had one that was bendy, could we do anything about it? Feel down the middle of your back. What can you feel? Look at the picture of the skeleton* (Photocopiable Thinksheet 19 on page 78). *What have you been feeling? That's the backbone. It's a bit like a broom handle. See how it's made of lots of small bones? What difference does that make?*

Step 4d: Arm and leg bones

Our arm and leg bones are hollow tubes. Classroom chair and table legs are often made from tubular materials. Have such an item to hand. Discuss the lightness and strength of the legs. Relate these to the function of the arm and leg bones. (Photocopiable Thinksheet 19 shows the arm and leg bones.)

Talk: *Look at this chair. See its legs – are they strong or weak? Can they take a lot of weight? If I were to saw across one of the legs, what would I find? The legs are hollow, yet they still work. What difference would it make if they were solid? Would the chair be lighter or heavier? Would it have needed more steel to make the chair? Look at the skeleton's legs in the picture. How are they like chair legs? What about the arm bones? Why are they like that?*

More to talk about and do

Links with structures and mechanisms in Design and Technology

This is an occasion where work in science can lead very naturally into work in D&T and vice versa. Bicycles, skyscrapers, bridges, boats and ships all have frameworks to support them, give them strength and help them keep their intended shape. Tudor houses often have fairly obvious wooden frameworks, as do dwellings on stilts. The lower jaw is an example of a hinged joint, like a loose version of a hinged pencil box lid. The hip joint is a ball and socket joint. This allows a greater freedom of movement than a hinge joint. Talk about the parallels with the children.

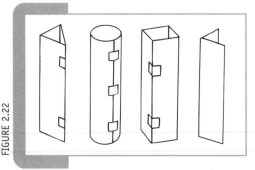

FIGURE 2.22

Hands-on: testing shapes for their strength

Empty eggshells can be put into an eggcup and loaded with weights. Children are often surprised at how much weight such a 'fragile', helmet-shaped object will take before it collapses. The strength of various shapes made from paper can be tested fairly readily (Figure 2.22). This also provides an opportunity for children to practise planning and carrying out a fair test.

Checking for understanding

Check on the children's understanding with questions and tasks, such as:
▶ *What would you look like without a skeleton? Why?*
▶ *How can your arm move in different directions?*
▶ *Invent a new skeleton for yourself. It should do something you cannot do. Tell me what it can do and how it can do that.*

Related topics
▶ Forces (page 124).

Animals

Same and different

1 Compare animal neighbours. How is a person like a chimpanzee? How is a chimpanzee like a bear? Work your way around the animals anticlockwise, until you have compared a grasshopper and a fly. Then think about how a fly is like a person.

2 How is a person different to a chimpanzee? How is a chimpanzee different to a bear? Work your way around the animals again, until you have done the grasshopper and the fly. Then think about how a fly is different to a person.

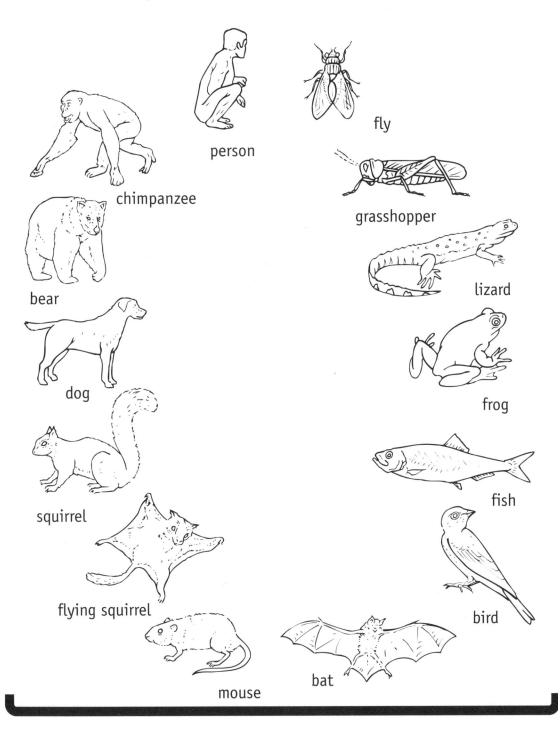

fly

person

chimpanzee

grasshopper

bear

lizard

dog

frog

squirrel

fish

flying squirrel

bird

mouse

bat

Changes in animals

Baby animals that grow up

These are baby animals. The first one is an elephant.

1 What are the others?

2 Draw a picture of a grown-up elephant next to the baby elephant.

3 Look at the other animals. What would the grown-ups look like? Draw their pictures next to the baby animals.

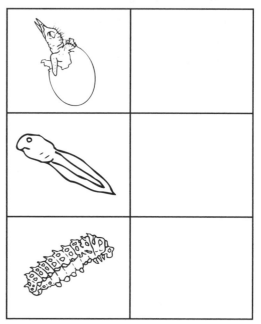

4 This is a grown-up cow. What did she look like when she was a baby cow? Draw your picture in the empty box.

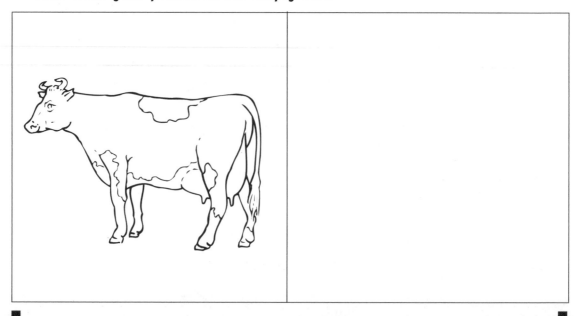

How do plants change?

The first picture shows you what this plant looked like in the spring.
The last picture shows you what it looked like in the autumn.
The box in the middle is for what the plant looked like in the summer.

1 Draw what you think it would look like in the summer. There is an empty box for you to put your picture in (number 3).
2 Now draw what you think it would look like just after spring but just before summer. Put your picture in box number 2.
3 Now draw what you think it would look like just after summer but before autumn. Put your picture in box number 4.
4 Underneath these pictures, explain why you made your pictures look like they do.

SPRING		SUMMER		AUTUMN
 1	2	3	4	 5

a) I made picture 3 look like this because

_____

b) I made picture 2 look like this because

_____

c) I made picture 4 look like this because

_____

Changes in plants

Robby the robot eats his breakfast

Digestion

Robby cannot eat as we do. He has to do all his eating on the outside. The picture shows how he eats and gets the goodness out of things.
Robby needs bits and pieces to keep him in good repair. Computers and things like that are put on the conveyor belt for him.

1 Find the computers and things like that on the conveyor belt.
2 The conveyor belt moves them along to a big, bouncy hammer. This begins to break them up.
Where do we begin to break our food up?
3 After that, some oil is dripped on the bits to loosen the nuts and bolts. The chunks fall apart and are even smaller now.
Where do we break up food into a sloppy mess?
4 Robby picks out the bits he needs and stores them inside himself for later.
Where do we take out the useful parts from what we eat?
5 The bits that Robby does not want move on along the conveyor belt. The left-over oil is sucked out and sent back to the oil can so it can be used again.
Where do we take out useful water from what is left of our food?
6 Finally, the unwanted bits fall off the conveyor belt into the bin.
I am sure I do not have to ask you if we do something like that ourselves.

Things that live together

You have a chance to fly in a spaceship. You land on another world and find lots of living things. You have never seen anything like them before, so you give them names. You call one kind of living thing a 'tramblegrot'. Tramblegrots are everywhere. You call another kind a 'dobble'. There are not many dobbles. Rarest of all is a kind of living thing you call a 'biddlebat'. You only see two in the whole day. You do see more of another kind. You call these 'pluttsos'. As you are a good scientist, you draw pictures of what these look like and make a note of how many you see. Complete the table by drawing pictures.

What it looked like	What you called it	How many you saw
	a tramblegrot	2381
	a dobble	8
	a biddlebat	2
	a pluttso	17

1 Arrange these living things into a food chain. Draw a picture of your food chain here.

2 Explain how you decided how to arrange these living things into a food chain.

3 If these living things had been on Earth, what might a tramblegrot be?

4 What might a biddlebat be on Earth?

SCHOLASTIC
Photocopiable

Feeding relationships

Green plants

Plants: same and different

Look at these plants.

1 **Start with the lettuce plant. How is it like the radish?**
2 **How is the radish like the onion plant?**
3 **How is the onion plant like the grass plant?**
4 **How is the grass plant like the elder bush?**
5 **How is the elder bush like the beech tree?**
6 **How is the beech tree like the fir tree?**
7 **How is the fir tree like the lettuce?**

lettuce

fir tree

radish

beech tree

onion

elder bush

grass

SCHOLASTIC TEACHER BOOKSHOP
Teaching Tricky Science Concepts

SCHOLASTIC
Photocopiable

The ear bones: the smallest bones in your body

Hearing

There are three tiny bones in your ear. They are the smallest bones in your body. Their job is to make the tiny movements of the eardrum bigger. You can see how they work for yourself. This is what to do:

1 Place this sheet of paper on a sheet of cardboard.
2 Ask your teacher for a plastic straw, five pins and some safe scissors.
3 Cut three pieces off the straw to match the ones in the picture.
4 Lie the pieces of straw on top of the pieces in the picture.
5 Use three of your pins. Push them right through the straws at the places marked X.
6 Use the other two pins to join the straws together at the places marked Y. Push these pins through the straw ends to join them. Do not push them into the paper or card.

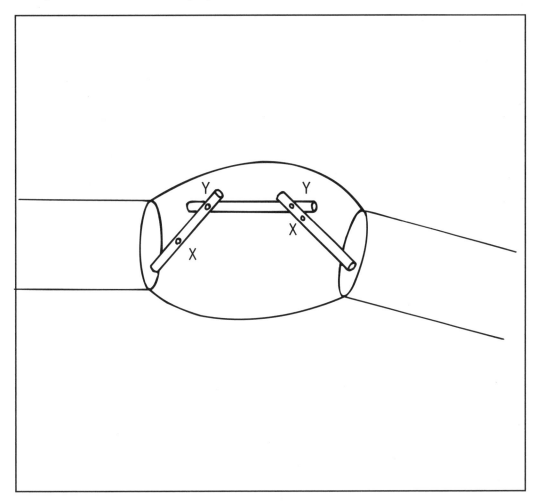

7 Watch what happens when you move the end of the straw that touches the eardrum. Make it move only a small amount. What does the straw at the other end do? Does it move more?

Life

Alive or not alive?

Look at these pictures. Some of them show living things. Some of them show things that are not living.

Which pictures show living things? Do they move, eat, excrete (poop), grow, breathe and have young ones? If they do, then they are probably alive. Write *Alive* under the ones you think are alive.

The out-of-sight world of microbes

Microbes

Microbes are everywhere. They even float around in the air you breathe.

1 Copy these pictures of microbes on to thin card and cut them out.

2 Colour them.

3 Ask your teacher to hang them by threads in the classroom to remind people that microbes are everywhere, even in the air.

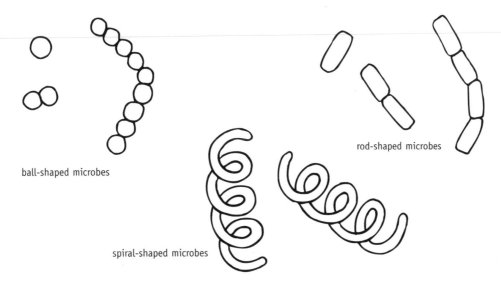

ball-shaped microbes

rod-shaped microbes

spiral-shaped microbes

Useful microbes and compost-making

Microbes turn leaves and other parts of plants into compost. Compost has lots of materials in it that plants need to grow. This means that compost is good for the garden. Gardeners can make their own compost from garden waste. This picture shows how they do it.

1 How do the pipes with holes in them help the microbes?

2 The gardener has to sprinkle water on the compost heap from time to time. Why does this help the microbes?

3 Which part of the year do you think is best for compost making?

4 Why?

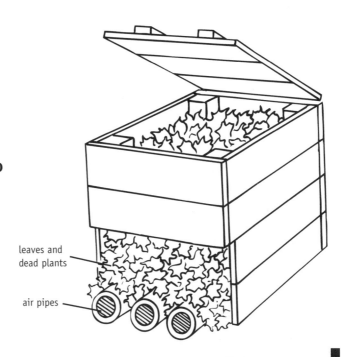

leaves and dead plants

air pipes

Bones and more bones

This picture shows what the bones inside us look like. It cannot show all the bones we have. Some are too small to show. How many can you count?

skeleton

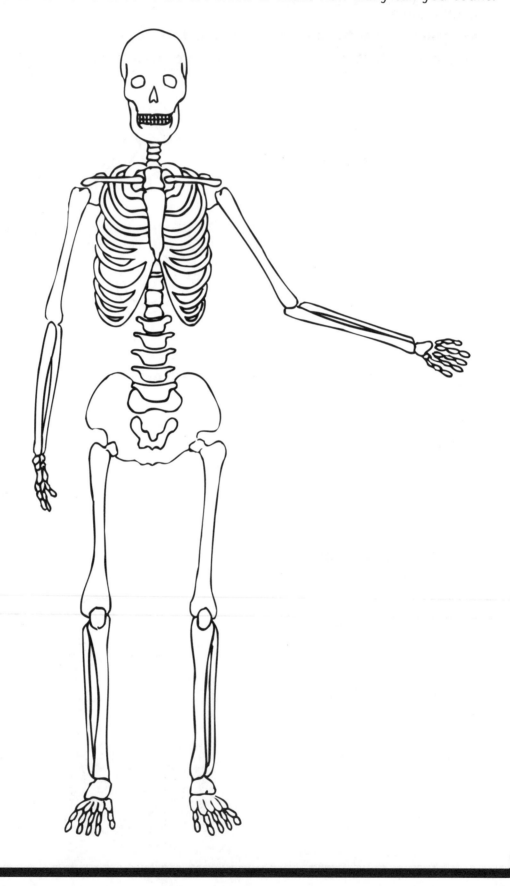

Chapter 3
Materials

This chapter gives you ways of helping children understand some aspects of materials. It deals with properties of materials and how materials can be grouped and changed. You will, of course, also have to teach about changes in the natural world (in animals and plants). These have been included in Chapter 2, but you could also introduce them here. While the topics in this part can be free-standing, you will be able to relate them to one another as you proceed. The topics in this chapter are organised alphabetically in order to make it easy to locate the one you want. Dip into them, select from them and adapt them to support your normal routine and to meet the needs of the children. The table below shows when the topics are likely to be useful.

Topic	When to use the topic
Changes	▶ when introducing changes in materials ▶ when talking about reversible and non-reversible changes ▶ when investigating changes with time.
Chemical changes	▶ when explaining the formation of new materials ▶ when explaining burning ▶ when investigating everyday, safe, chemical changes.
Dissolving	▶ when explaining changes produced by water ▶ when distinguishing dissolving from melting ▶ when investigating solubility.
Evaporation	▶ when explaining evaporation and condensation ▶ when talking about reversible changes ▶ when preparing children for understanding the water cycle.
Materials	▶ when exploring materials and their properties ▶ when teaching about ways of sorting and grouping materials according to their physical properties ▶ when preparing the way for learning about specific materials, such as rocks and soils.
Melting	▶ when explaining changes caused by heating materials ▶ when distinguishing melting from boiling.
Permeability	▶ when explaining and investigating the properties of common materials ▶ when teaching about rocks and soils ▶ when teaching about sources of water.
Soils	▶ when exploring the properties of materials (as a specific example) ▶ when teaching about the characteristics of rocks and soils ▶ when explaining the importance of natural materials ▶ when investigating the properties of natural materials.
Solids, liquids & gases	▶ when exploring the variety of materials ▶ when grouping materials ▶ when explaining the properties of materials.
Stretching	▶ when teaching about the elastic properties of materials and changes produced by forces ▶ when investigating changes due to compressing things and stretching things.

Changes

What is change?

Nothing is for ever; things change with time. Changes can be sudden (like snapping a pencil) or slow (like the movement of a clock's hands, the decay of a log, the accumulation of dust or the erosion of a mountain). Or they can be something in between (like the boiling of a kettle). Some changes are reversible (like denting a car and then having the dent knocked out); others are permanent (like making bread – there is no going back to the wheat, or even to the flour). Science is often about changes. There are physical changes, like those involved in melting or stretching materials. Many of these are reversible. There are also chemical changes, like those involved in rusting. These can be quite difficult to reverse and, for practical purposes, are generally treated as permanent.

Understanding changes

Young children, in particular, may think that most changes can be reversed, if not by them then by a competent adult. In addition, the continuous nature of some changes, like decay, may not be apparent to them. The aim is to help them see changes in the world around them and identify different kinds of change.

Steps to understanding

Direct experience provides food for thought and discussion. In these steps, it comes from some simple physical changes.

Age range and duration

The steps are suitable for most children and would take about an hour if done on one occasion, not including any written or other activities.

Step 1: Some permanent changes

You will need an old shoe and a relatively new shoe, a twig and length of thin wooden dowel, and a biscuit and some of its ingredients (for example, flour and sugar). Contrast the items in each pair and draw the children's attention to the permanent nature of the changes.

> **Talk:** (Reveal the new shoe.) *Look at this shoe. Is it an old shoe? How do you know?* (Reveal the old shoe.) *Is this an old shoe? If I left it overnight, would it look as good as new tomorrow? Even if I polished it, would it look as good as the new one? It's changed, hasn't it? We'll never make it new again. It's changed for ever and can never be changed back. It's permanently changed. Here's something different.* (Compare the twig and length of wood, and the biscuit and its ingredients in the same way.) *Look at this biscuit. Do you know what it's made from? These are some of the things that went into it. They were mixed together, spread on a baking tray and put into an oven. Have they been changed for ever? Could we get them back from the biscuit? Can you think of another change that is for ever, a permanent change?*

Step 2: Some temporary changes

This step focuses on temporary changes. Begin with a ball of clay. After that, you will need a large elastic band or similar item, a flexible twig, a spring (for example, a slinky spring) and a bar of chocolate. Take each in turn, change it and show that it can be returned to its original state.

Talk: *Look at this modelling clay. What shape is it? Watch, I'm going to flatten it. Can I make it go back to being ball-shaped? Do it for me. Let's make something else. Can I make that go back to the ball shape? Whatever I do, I can always make it go back to what it was. (Reveal the elastic band.) What's this? How could I change it? Watch, I'll stretch it (hold it extended). Will it stay stretched? What will happen if I let it go? Was it permanently stretched? No, it was a temporary change. That means it goes back to what it was before. Look at this twig. Watch, I'm bending it. Is that a permanent change or a temporary change? Why do you think that? How can we see if you are right? (Show the spring.) What about this? Can we use this to make a temporary change? How could we do it? Can you think of another temporary change? (Extend the discussion by showing the chocolate and softening a piece of it on a saucer over a radiator. Let it cool and solidify to illustrate another kind of temporary change – solid to liquid to solid.)*

Step 3: Using new ideas

You will need an apple. The aim is to discuss three changes, all permanent. The first (cutting the apple in half) is a quick change. The second (going brown) is a slower change. The third, decay, is a much slower process. Ask the children to tell you what happens to an apple if it is left a long time. It will not, of course, decay in the short interval after cutting it, and it would be unwise to leave it to decay for health and safety reasons. Photocopiable Thinksheet 20 on page 105 will help you develop this step futher.

Talk: *Look, I'm cutting the apple in half. Have I changed it? Could I make it like it was? I can put it together, but will it heal as though it had never been cut? What colour is it inside? Can you see it changing? What colour is that? So, it's going brown. Is that a change? Is it for ever? If I left the apple for a really long time, what would happen then? Would you still eat it? Why not?*

More to talk about and do

Limits to change

Even temporary changes have their limits. Stretch the elastic band repeatedly and it will not return exactly to what it was. If the spring is a metal one and you overstretch it, the extension will be permanent. Many changes to the human body would be permanent if it were not for our ability to repair ourselves. The elastic band and spring cannot do that.

FIGURE 3.1

Hands-on: growing things

The growth of a plant from a seed is more obvious with a large seed, such as a broad bean. The children could grow and examine these. Similarly, an amaryllis, once started, grows remarkably quickly and produces a spectacular flower with very little need for attention (see Figure 3.1).

Checking for understanding

Check on the children's understanding with questions and tasks, such as:
▶ *Tell me what 'permanent' change means. How is it different to a 'temporary' change?*
▶ *If I knit a sweater with this ball of wool, what kind of change would it be? Why do you think that?*
▶ *If I let my lollipop melt, is that a permanent or a temporary change? Why do you think that?*

Related topics
▶ Stretching (page 102)
▶ Chemical changes (page 82)
▶ Solids, liquids and gases (page 99).

Chemical changes

What is a chemical change?

A chemical change is not like a physical change. In physical changes, the material stays the same. For example, when you chop up some modelling clay, it is still clay. If you warm some chocolate, it becomes runny but it is still chocolate. In chemical changes, the material itself changes. For example, if milk goes sour, it is not milk any more. Bacteria have changed it into something that behaves, smells and tastes quite different. If you add water to baking powder, it froths and fizzes. Afterwards, it is no longer baking powder and will not froth and fizz again. If you leave a new iron nail outside for a few days, it will rust. Tiny pieces of iron join up with particles from damp air and make brown iron oxide. Rust does not behave like iron. For example, iron will let electricity through it but rust will not. A rusty nail has to be cleaned before it can be used in an electrical circuit.

Understanding chemical change

It may be difficult to know when a chemical change has taken place simply by watching. For example, has the iron changed into rust or did the rust come entirely from the air, like dust? The aim is to make children aware of the existence of chemical changes, and help them come to understand that different materials are formed.

Steps to understanding

Using simple and safe materials, these steps make the child aware of chemical change. They include an analogy to help the children grasp the nature of the change.

Age range and duration

Chemical change is generally better understood by older children in the primary school. Steps 1 and 2 will need about an hour. Parts of Step 3, observing chemical changes, will involve waiting time, so you could include other activities or written work during that time.

Step 1: The scarecrow who can change

This analogy aims to highlight the contrast between changes that leave things essentially the same (like physical changes) and those that change them radically (like chemical changes). Worzel is a rather timid scarecrow with a turnip for a head. If he changes his clothes or becomes wet in the rain or hot in the sun, he is still Worzel (changes that leave timid Worzel still timid Worzel). But Worzel can change parts of his body. When he does, he becomes someone new. For instance, he has another head that changes him into a brave and confident scarecrow (rather like the new things produced by a chemical change). See Photocopiable Thinksheet 21 on page 106 for help with this step.

> **Talk:** (Explain who Worzel is and illustrate ways in which he can change: changes that make no real difference, and changes that make a big differences so that Worzel needs a new name.) *Is he still Worzel? Why not? Does he need a new name?*

Step 2: Chemical change: before and after

The purpose of this step is to help children notice the radical effect of chemical change. You will need at least one, and preferably more than one, of: a slice of bread and a slice of cold, overdone toasted bread; a new iron object and a heavily corroded iron object (like a nail or bolt); a fresh egg and a hard boiled egg. Taking each in turn, ask the children to compare and contrast the substances. (Do not let children handle or taste raw egg because of a risk of microbes such as salmonella.)

Talk: *Look at this slice of bread. What does it feel like? Does it have a smell? What colour is it? What's this?* (Show the toasted bread.) *What did it look like to start with? How is it different to the bread? Watch, I'm scraping off some of the black stuff. Is that anything like the bread? Could we change it back to bread? Do you know what this is?* (Show the corroded nail.) *What was it to start with? How is it different to the new nail? Watch, I'm scraping some of the brown stuff off. Is it anything like the iron? How is it different? You all know what this is.* (Show the fresh, uncooked egg.) *What's it like inside?* (Break the egg into a bowl.) *How is it different to this?* (Show the hard-boiled egg.) *It's hard boiled. Tell me what it's like inside. How is it different from the other egg?* (Break open the hard boiled egg and compare it with the other egg.) *The bread has changed into something different – this black stuff. This black stuff is not bread any more. The nail has changed into something different – this rust. The rust is not iron any more.*

Step 3: Watching chemical changes

You will need:

- some baking powder in a clear plastic bottle without a lid
- some water
- a potato
- a knife
- three or four, clean, grease-free nails
- plastic pots containing damp cotton wool or blotting paper (see Figure 3.2).

FIGURE 3.2

These will illustrate a fast chemical change (by adding drops of water to the baking powder), a slower chemical change (by cutting the potato so it goes brown when part of the air reacts with it), and a slow chemical change (as nails rust when placed on damp cotton wool in air – remember to keep the cotton wool damp).

Talk: *I'm going to show you some changes that are like Worzel changing his head. They all make something different. Watch. I'm going to put a few drops of water on the baking powder. Look, I'll do it again. What happens? Was it quick or slow? What has happened to the baking powder? Is it still baking powder? Look at this potato. I'm cutting it in half. What colour is it? Let's just leave it for a moment. Look at these nails. What are they made of? Are they rusty? Look, this is cotton wool. I'm making it damp and I've put the nails on them. We'll leave them for a while. What do you think will happen? What's happened to the potato? Was it fast or slow? Look at the nails. Have they gone rusty yet? No, not yet. We'll have to keep looking at them. Do you think they will change quickly or slowly?*

More to talk about and do

Burning as a chemical change

This is a talk-about activity and does not involve the actual burning of materials. The chemical changes involved in making toast are due to burning. Burning is when a substance (bread in this case) combines with oxygen in the air. There are chemical changes that go on in our bodies. For instance, our bodies take in air and use some of its oxygen to burn food. This burning is very slow, but it is enough to keep us warm. Rusting is another example of very slow burning as iron combines with oxygen in the air. Water and baking powder, however, do not burn. They combine and make a gas that makes the water frothy.

Hands-on: how can we prevent iron rusting?

Ask the children to begin a list of things that are made of iron (and steel, a form of iron). The list should soon become long. We depend on iron a lot, so we do not want it to rust away. What makes it rust? How can we prevent it rusting? Ask the children to design and try an experiment to test their ideas (Figure 3.3).

Checking for understanding
Check on the children's understanding with questions and tasks, such as:

▶ *The shed is on fire! It is made of wood and it burns down before the fire-engine arrives. When it is finished, there are only blackened ashes. What do you think? Is this like Worzel changing his clothes or changing his head? Why do you think that?*

▶ *Here is some wheat. Do you know what is made from it? Here is some flour. That's a change. Is this like Worzel changing his clothes or changing his head? Why do you think that? What can you make from flour? Here's a loaf of bread. That's another change. Is this like Worzel changing his clothes or changing his head? Why do you think that?*

▶ *If you forget about the milk, what happens to it? Could you change it back into fresh milk? Why do you think that?*

FIGURE 3.3

I think rubbing it with soap will protect it because ...

I would try milk. Milk might work because ...

What about colouring it with a felt-tip pen? I think that will work because ...

Related topics
▶ Changes (page 80)
▶ Changes in animals (page 42)
▶ Changes in plants (page 44)
▶ Melting (page 92)
▶ Stretching (page 102)
▶ Dissolving (page 84)
▶ Evaporation (page 86).

Dissolving

· ·

What is dissolving?
Dissolving is what happens when something is added to a liquid and becomes a part of it so that we can no longer distinguish it from the liquid. The blend is called a *solution*. For example, a little sugar stirred in water will disappear to leave a clear solution of sweet-tasting water. The dissolved sugar can be reclaimed by leaving the solution to evaporate. The water escapes into the air leaving the sugar behind. While some materials dissolve readily in water, a lot do not. Glass, for instance, does not dissolve in water, which is why we use it in windows where it is exposed to the rain. Roofing tiles, bricks and umbrellas behave similarly. Some substances mix with water but do not really dissolve. Instead, they form little bits that can be seen floating in a diluted version of the liquid. Milk and some paints are like that.

Understanding dissolving
Dissolving may be confused with melting. A dissolving sugar cube, for instance, may look a little like a melting piece of butter or chocolate. Additionally, the word *melting* is often used loosely to refer to the process of *dissolving*. The aim is to help children understand the process of dissolving in a way that helps them distinguish it from other processes, such as melting.

Steps to understanding
▶ The first step provides direct experience of dissolving.
▶ The second step explores the process further.
▶ The third step introduces an analogy to help children grasp the nature of dissolving.

Age range and duration

The steps are suitable for both younger and older children. Step 1 will need about half an hour and is suitable for very young children. Putting aside additional time for written or other tasks, the other steps may need a further hour if taken on one occasion.

Step 1: Observing dissolving

Provide the children with a plastic cup and spoon, some water in the cup and some coloured sugar crystals. Ask them to taste a sugar crystal or two and confirm that they taste sweet. Next, ask the children to taste a few drops of the water and confirm that it is not sweet. They should now put a spoonful of sugar crystals into the water and watch what happens to them. Finally, ask the children to stir the water until all the crystals have dissolved, then taste a drop of the solution.

Talk: *What do the crystals of sugar look like? Have you seen anything that looks like that before? What does a crystal of sugar taste like? What is happening to the sugar crystals? What does the water drop taste like? What do you think has happened to the sugar?*

FIGURE 3.4

Step 2: Where has the sugar gone?

Ask the children to repeat the first step but this time, they should weigh the water, weigh the sugar and weigh the solution (Figure 3.4).

Talk: *What happened to the sugar? Did it really disappear? How do we know it is still in the water? Why does the water weigh more afterwards? How much more does it weigh? Where did this extra weight come from?*

Step 3: Introducing an analogy for dissolving

You will need several small balloons, fastened loosely together in pairs, and a bin of polystyrene chips or loops (as used in packing). This provides a large-scale analogy that is easy to see in a classroom. Show the children the pairs of balloons, piled up like the piles of sugar crystals. Let them see the bin of loops. (Do not let the children play with them or have access to them; they can be messy and they may try to chew or swallow one.) This bin represents the cup of water. Gently begin to submerge a pair of balloons (a tiny bit of 'sugar') in the bin of 'water'. As the 'water' flows around and between the balloons, unfasten them so that they drift apart in the 'water'. Add another pair, and another and so on until you have an even mix of dissolved 'sugar' in 'water' (see Figure 3.5).

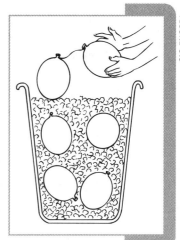

FIGURE 3.5

Talk: *Look, these balloons are going to be our sugar. This is the cup and this is the water* (running your hands amongst the loops; you should warn the children of the dangers of chewing and swallowing these and similar items). *I'm going to put some sugar into the water. Watch how the water gets everywhere and, look, it's loosening the string; the sugar is breaking apart and floating off. Here's another one. What do you think will happen? See how the sugar has broken apart and it's all mixed up with the water. This is a little bit like what happened in your cups. It's not exactly the same, though. Can you tell me some ways that it is different? Why did the sugar-water you made weigh more than the water you started with?*

More to talk about and do

Is dissolving a good thing?

Talk with the children about how it can be useful to have things that dissolve. For instance, it makes it possible for us to get the nutrients we need from our food. On the other hand, for D&T, we often want things that will not dissolve, such as cups, roof tiles and clothes. However, this can be a real problem. Take, for instance, plastic cups, carrier bags and old tyres. They can make the place a mess and be hard to dispose of. No amount of rain will dissolve them. This is why biodegradable plastics have been produced. Some cups and bags last long enough for what you want, then slowly break down.

Hands-on: there are limits to dissolving

There is a limit to the amount of sugar that will dissolve in a cup of water. Give the children a small plastic cup of water. (A small cup of water will take less sugar to saturate it than a large cup.)

Talk: *How many level teaspoons of sugar will dissolve in it? Will it go on for ever? What do you think? Why do you think that? Let's try it; do one spoonful at a time. Do not add another until the last one has completely gone.*

Photocopiable Thinksheet 22 on page 107 could be used here. It asks the children to apply what they know about dissolving.

Checking for understanding

Check on the children's understanding with questions and tasks, such as:

▶ *Draw what sugary water might look like if your eyes were like very powerful magnifiers.*
▶ *William was sent to the shop. He had to buy a bag of sugar and a bottle of pop. 'These are heavy!' he complained. 'I know what I'll do! I'll dissolve the sugar in the pop, then I won't have to carry the sugar.' What do you think? Is this good thinking? Why do you think that?*
▶ *Joan keeps bees so she can collect the honey that they make. In the spring, the bees wake up and are hungry and thirsty. Joan usually gives them sugary water to drink. She puts some sugar in a bottle of water and shakes it. She can still see some sugar in the water. What can she do to try to make more sugar dissolve? Why do you think your idea would work?*

Related topics
▶ Changes (page 80)
▶ Melting (page 92)
▶ Evaporation (page 86).

Evaporation
· ·

What is evaporation?

Evaporation is the change of a liquid into a *vapour* as the tiny particles of the liquid escape from its surface. For example, a pool of water on a kitchen worktop will slowly disappear as the water evaporates into the air. This happens at all temperatures, but is generally faster when the water is warm. Evaporation can also be faster if the air is moving, as when the kitchen window is open. Moving air can carry the tiny particles away and the pool soon disappears. (This is also why washing often dries quickly on a warm and windy day.) On the other hand, if the kitchen is kept closed, the water vapour in the air may build up and make the room feel humid. In this case, a pool of water can last a long time.

Understanding evaporation

There is often nothing much to see when a pool of water evaporates, and children often develop their own theories about what happens. For instance, some may believe that the water disappears, quite literally. Others may think it soaks into the surface. Another view is that water is sucked up by the sun. You could try to show that such ideas are not sound. For instance, water in a cup in a dark cupboard still disappears even though there is no sunlight. But this still leaves the problem of what *does* happen to the water. The aim is to help children understand the process of evaporation and how it can lead to drying.

Steps to understanding
It helps if you give the children something they can see and think with. These steps aim to do that. Each one focuses on the evaporation of water, the liquid most familiar to children. Each step also prepares the child for the next step.

Age range and duration
The concept of evaporation is generally better understood by older children in the primary school. The sequence will take between one and two hours to complete, putting aside time for written and other activities.

FIGURE 3.6

Step 1: What happens to the water in a wet towel?
Show a wet towel and ask what happens to the water in it when it is hung on the washing line to dry. You may be able to add some contradictory thoughts to some of the children's ideas.

Talk: *So you think that the sun sucks out the water? What if you hung the towel where there was no sun: would it still dry? Let's try it with this wet handkerchief.*

Step 2: Making evaporating water visible
Put the towel aside and take a dish of warm water. Stand the dish in a cold place or outside on a cold day. The vapour leaving the surface of the water will be visible as a mist (Figure 3.6).

Talk: *Look just above the water; what can you see? What is it? Why is it doing that? If we leave it for a long time, what do you think will happen? Have you seen anything else do this?*

FIGURE 3.7

Step 3: Making invisible water vapour visible
Place a dish of water indoors, next to a cold window. The vapour will form a film of water on the glass. The children may need time to convince themselves that the water on the window has come from the dish. This will involve discussion (Figure 3.7).

Talk: *What's happening on the glass? Where is it coming from? You think it's coming from the dish? How could we check that? Take the dish away and see if it still happens. Bring it back; has it started again? What is it?*

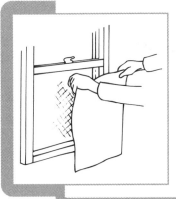
FIGURE 3.8

Step 4: Showing that a wet towel gives off water vapour
Hold the wet towel near the cold window and let the children see the film of water that forms on the glass. Invite them to explain where it has come from and what is happening to the water in the towel (Figure 3.8).

Talk: *What's happening on the window? What does it remind you of? Why is that? What's making the window do that? Where is it coming from? Would it happen if the towel was dry? Why do you think that?*

FIGURE 3.9

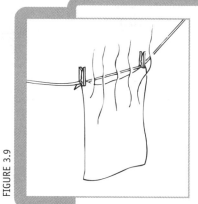

Step 5: Showing that a wet towel on a clothes line gives off water vapour

Hang the towel outside and, if it is a cold day, the water vapour leaving the towel will be visible as a drifting mist. Alternatively, you could make the water vapour visible by placing the wet towel in the open doorway of a cold refrigerator (Figure 3.9).

Talk: *Look at the towel; what is happening? Where is the mist coming from? When will it stop doing that? How would we know if the towel is drying without feeling it?*

More to talk about and do
Vocabulary: condensation and boiling

Condensation is the reverse of evaporation. Having established the concept of evaporation, you need to introduce the word *condensation* and, for instance, link it to what happens on windows on cold days. Boiling can be confused with evaporation. Unlike evaporation, boiling generally starts near the source of heat and spreads throughout the water, producing bubbles of steam. It happens at only one temperature, about 100°C in the case of water. Both evaporation and boiling reduce the amount of liquid water, although evaporation generally takes longer. For safety, you would not have children boil water, but it is useful if you distinguish between evaporation and boiling by talking about it.

Hands-on: will it dry faster if we spread it out?

If water is spread out to make a large pool, it will dry faster than if it is kept in a small pool. Evaporation increases as the surface area of the water increases, all else being equal. Using a straw, place a drop of water on a plastic plate. Next to that, place another drop and spread it a little to make a bigger pool. Then place another drop on the plate and spread it out to make the largest pool. Ask the children which one will dry (evaporate) the fastest. Also ask them to justify their responses. Have them test their ideas practically using water, a straw and plastic plates (see also Photocopiable Thinksheet 23 on page 108).

Hands-on: finding out what happens to a warm pool

Generally, the warmer the liquid, the faster it evaporates. This is because the bits of water are moving faster in the warmer liquid and are more likely to break through the surface and escape. The children can see this for themselves by comparing what happens to a drop of water on a plastic plate on a cold table with what happens to a matching drop on a plate on a warm radiator. (Some children are happy to test this using only one plate placed on a radiator. You may have to discuss the need for a second plate on the table to compare it with. The second task on Photocopiable Thinksheet 23 will help you do that.)

Related topics
▶ Solids, liquids and gases (page 99)
▶ Dissolving (page 84).

Checking for understanding

Check on the children's understanding with questions and tasks, such as:
▶ *What kind of weather is best for hanging out washing? Why?*
▶ *If we put a wet towel into a plastic bag and close the top of the bag, will the towel dry? Why is that?*
▶ *Soil in a garden can dry out quickly, leaving the plants' roots without water. Gardeners sometimes spread grass cuttings or bark on the surface of the soil (a mulch). The soil stays damp under the cuttings or bark for a long time. Why?*

Materials

Types of material
Materials can be sorted in a variety of ways, including:
- appearance – for example, shiny or dull (such as *cooking foil* or *blotting paper*)
- feel – for example, rough or smooth to the touch (such as *sandpaper* or a *mirror*)
- origin – for example, natural or artificial (such as *wood* or *plastic*)
- use – for example, building or clothing (such as *brick* or *cotton*)
- state – solid, liquid or a gas (such as *stone, water, air*)
- ability to conduct electricity – that is, conductor or insulator (such as *copper* or *wood*)
- density – that is, how heavy or light it is for its size (such as *a house brick* or *a cinder block*)
- living or non-living (such as *a dog* or *a stone*).

Each way of sorting materials depends on the characteristic or property you have chosen.

The problem with understanding the sorting of materials
Materials present several problems for children. First, young children tend to think of the object rather than the material (a *spoon* rather than the *plastic* or *metal* of which it is made). Second, children can have difficulty with the word *material*. They may have heard the word used to refer to fabrics and so be confused by the way you use it. Third, children do not always distinguish between materials with ease. Fourth, the property you want them to use to sort materials may also be poorly understood. On occasions, you may find that children begin sorting according to one property (for example, shiny–dull) and drift to another (rough–smooth). The aim is for children to learn some properties of common materials, to sort them accordingly and to use the term *material* appropriately.

Steps to understanding
- The first two steps require children to use senses to identify some properties of materials and sort objects accordingly.
- The third step focuses on materials and the meaning of the term.
- Subsequent steps help children become familiar with different materials and ways of sorting them.

Age range and duration
The first two steps suit the experience of the youngest children. Allow up to an hour for them if taken on one occasion. With older children, you could proceed quickly through these initial steps and give at least an hour to the subsequent steps, putting aside time for written and other activities. You may want to reserve the final step (showing that materials can be classified in two ways at the same time) for the older children.

Step 1: Sorting by appearance
You need trays of objects (kept out of sight until you use them). One could be a mix of large and small versions of objects (for example, marble, ball; pencil box, shoe box). Another could be a mix of shiny and dull items (for example, cooking foil, sugar paper; plastic mirror, piece of card). A third could be a mix of transparent and opaque objects (a square piece cut from a clear plastic bag, a similar piece cut from a white plastic bag; a clear sweet paper, an opaque sweet paper). You also need two empty trays or something similar. Show the first tray of objects and contrast the items, as shown overleaf.

Talk: *What are these? Look, I'm going to put this into here* (placing the marble on one of the empty trays) *and this into here* (placing the ball on the other empty tray). *Which tray do you think this will this go on?* (Show the pencil box.) *What about this?* (Show the shoe box.) Divide all the objects into large and small. Have the children look for things in the classroom that they can add. *How did we know what to put in here? What about all the things in here? So we've sorted them out into big and small.* (Continue in the same way with the other trays of items.)

Step 2: Sorting by feel

This time, your trays of objects are to be sorted according to feel. One could be a mix of heavy and light objects (for example, a paperweight, a crumpled ball of paper). Another could be a mix of rough and smooth objects (for example, sandpaper, sheet of writing paper) or items that feel warm or cold to the touch (for example, woollen glove, pan lid). You also need two empty trays or something similar. Proceed as in Step 1.

Talk: *What are these? Look, I'm going to put this into here* (placing the paperweight onto one of the empty trays) *and this into here* (placing the crumpled ball of paper onto the other empty tray). *Which tray do you think this will this go on?* (Show another heavy object.) *What about this?* (Showing a light object.) In this way, divide the objects into heavy and light. Ask the children to look for things in the classroom that they can add. *How did we know what to put on here? What about all the things on here? So we've sorted them out into heavy and light.* (Continue in the same way with the other trays of items.)

Step 3: Same thing, different materials

You need something made in a wide range of materials (for example, spoons made of wood, metal, plastic, pot). Introduce the word *material*. Show the range of items to the children and ask what material they are made from. Extend this to identify the materials used in common classroom items (for example, eraser, door, handle, window, radiator, vase). Next, ask the children to look at the materials in the things they possess (coins, badges, shoes, pencils, sweaters, blouses). Make the point that, although we use the word *material* in connection with fabrics, it covers more than that.

Talk: *Look at these spoons. Are they all the same? What's different about them? Do you know what this one is made of? What material is this one made of?* (And so on.) In connection with classroom materials: *Can you tell me something made from the material, rubber? Can you tell me something made from the material, wood? What is this material?* (Indicate a window pane.) In connection with themselves: *What is in your pocket? What material is it made from? Is it made from just one material or more than one? What are they? What about your pocket? Is it a material? What material is it? What about your sweater? Does it have a label? Does the label tell you what materials it's made from?*

Step 4: Different things, different materials

For this step, you need a mixture of common objects (for example, metal fork, plastic cup, wooden spoon, pebble, book, eraser, cork stopper, leather bag, metal bolt, plastic ruler, wooden box). These are to be sorted into groups such as: metals, plastics, wood, stone, cork, leather. Avoid mixtures of materials in this step.

Talk: *What is this made of? What makes you think that? OK, start a 'Metals' pile there. Are there any more things made of metal?* (And so on.)

Step 5: Why use those materials?
This step deals with objects made from a range of materials (for example, pencil, pencil sharpener, pen, stapler, zip-fastened pencil bag). The materials used in each of these are to be identified. Discuss what makes each one suitable for its purpose.

Talk: *You all know what this is, don't you? How many different materials are there in it? What are they? Why use wood? What makes wood a good material to use? Is there another material that might be just as good? What makes it just as good?*

Step 6: Two-way classification
This final step shows children that materials can be sorted by two properties at the same time (for example, shiny or dull; cold to touch or warm to touch). You need a collection of objects. You could begin with the story of the time you went to the shop to buy a loaf of bread. The bread could be brown or white, sliced or uncut at the same time. So, you could have bought four different loaves of bread:

	Sliced	Uncut
White Brown	white sliced brown sliced	white uncut brown uncut

Next, turn the children's attention to the collection of objects. Can they be sorted in two ways at once? There will probably be several possibilities.

Talk: *What is one way we could sort these things? Is there another way? Can we do both at once? We'll need to keep ourselves organised, so let's draw a table.* (The one below is a possibility.)

	Feels cold	Feels warm
Shiny Dull		

More to talk about and do
Sorting materials by uses and by origin
We also sort materials by use. For instance, there are building materials, clothing materials and bedding materials. Ask the children to list specific materials under each heading and tell you why they are suited to their task. Also ask: *Could we find this material out there, somewhere? Does it grow; could we dig it up?* Some materials are more durable than others. Iron will eventually rust (we paint it to prevent rusting) and wood eventually rots. *But what happens to things made of plastic?* Some seem to hang around forever and make the place a mess. This, of course, can be used to lead to talk about caring for the environment. Recycling materials reduces disposal problems and waste. The children may be familiar with waste materials that are sorted into glass (and according to colour), paper and aluminium (cans).

Hands-on: sorting aids

Children can sort a mixture of pebbles, gravel and sand according to size by hand. They can compare that with a mechanical sort using a garden sieve, followed by a colander and then a flour sieve. This is an exercise that can lead to work on rocks and soils.

Hands-on: caring for the environment

The children can do a survey of rubbish in the school playground. *What is the most common kind of material? What seems to hang around the longest?* You will need to warn the children not to pick up rubbish – this is an 'eyes only' task.

Checking for understanding

Check on the children's understanding with questions and tasks, such as:

▶ *What's the same about these things* (a collection of objects that share some properties, such as being smooth or being made of a plastic)?
▶ *Can you group the things in the picture? What is the same in each group?* (See Photocopiable Thinksheet 24 on page 109.)
▶ *Can you group the things in the picture a different way? What is the same in each group?* (See Photocopiable Thinksheet 24 on page 109).

Melting

What is melting?

Melting is the change we see when a solid is heated and turns into a liquid. The temperature at which this happens is the *melting point*. Melting tends to be something we can see, as when candle wax melts under the flame or when chocolate melts by the heat of your hand.

The problem with understanding melting

Melting is sometimes confused with other processes, particularly dissolving. To make matters worse, the term *melting* is sometimes used in everyday conversations to refer to the dissolving of, for instance, sugar in tea or coffee. The aim is for children to understand melting as a change that can be reversed and that does not materially alter the substance.

Steps to understanding

It can help if you give the children something to think with, so an analogy is used to explain melting.

Age range and duration

The steps are suitable for both younger and older children. Step 1 will need about half an hour and is suitable for very young children. The other steps may need an additional hour, not including time for written and other activities that you may include.

Step 1: Observing melting

Place ice on a saucer on a warm radiator. Ask the children to watch and describe what happens to the ice as it melts. Check and, if necessary, develop and practise descriptive vocabulary relating to the process (ice, ice cube, cold, hard, solid; melt, melting, molten; water, pool, runny, warm).

Talk: *What's this? (Ice.) Where do you think it came from? What's it feel like? (Place the ice on the saucer on the radiator.) Watch. What's happening to it? Why does that happen? Tell me some differences between ice and water. Will the water turn back into ice? Can we turn water into ice? How can water be made into ice?*

FIGURE 3.10

Step 2: Introducing an analogy for melting

You will need some plastic bricks from a construction kit that click together. Use them to build a small, simple house. Show the children the house. Hold the house up and turn it around. Let the children see that the press-stud connections between the bricks are strong enough to hold them together, whichever way you turn the house. Now show the children what happens when something melts. Pull the house apart. Place the pieces in a pile on a table as you break them off. Inevitably, as the pile grows, the loose pieces roll down, spread out and make a 'pool' of house bits (Figure 3.10).

Talk: *Melting is a bit like a house falling down. Watch. I've made a house with plastic bricks. I'll help it fall apart. There's one chunk; here's another, and another. Look at the pile of bits. What do you think will happen if I put more bits on the pile? Let's see if you are right. See how it spreads out and makes a 'pool' of bricks.*

Step 3: Using the analogy to explain melting

Place a piece of chocolate on a saucer on a warm radiator. Ask the children to watch the chocolate as it melts. Help them make connections between the house being broken into bits and producing a 'pool' and the way the bits of chocolate make a pool of runny chocolate. With the house, it was you who broke the bits off. With the chocolate, the heat did it.

Talk: Referring to the house analogy: *Let's see if the same thing happens when we melt some chocolate. Look, the piece of chocolate is just like a house. What's happening to it? It's much more runny than the house bricks. Is it making a runny pile? The house has bricks we can see. Can we see the chocolate's 'bricks'? Even though we can't see the 'bricks' in the chocolate, they do what the house bricks did. Once the heat loosens them, they run into a pool.*

Step 4: An important difference

Let the chocolate cool. Ask the children to confirm that the chocolate has become hard and solid again. Explain that the bits have joined together again, but not in the same way as before. This is not like the pool of plastic bricks. No matter how long we wait, the bits will never join together by themselves.

Talk: *Is the chocolate hard again? Is it solid? Is it still chocolate? What happened to the little bits that ran all over the plate? Have they joined up again? Have they made the shape we started with? Will our pile of house bits turn back into a house? (No.)*

More to talk about and do

Melting in nature

Talk about melting in nature. The example most familiar to children is likely to be the melting of ice and snow to form water. Ice cream and lollipops often melt before we have time to finish them. Butter and chocolate will also melt in the sun on a warm day. On a really hot day, even the tar on the road becomes sticky. Where it is really hot, inside the

Earth, rock will melt. When this molten rock runs from a volcano, it is called *lava*. Ask the children to think of and describe examples of melting. For instance, marshmallows will melt on hot drinking chocolate, butter or cheese on hot toast, tar on the road on a hot day, snow in sunshine, and ice lollipops in their mouths. In Design and Technology, the children may also have seen the solid 'glue' (a plastic) melt in a glue gun.

Related topics
▶ Solids, liquids and gases (page 99)
▶ Changes (page 80)
▶ Dissolving (page 84).

Hands-on: Nasir and the snowballs
Photocopiable Thinksheet 25 on page 110 tells a story and provides the results of an investigation for discussion. The children could try this for themselves using ice cubes.

Checking for understanding
Check on the children's understanding with questions and tasks, such as:
▶ *Suppose you were a tiny bit in a square of chocolate. Describe what would happen to you as your square of chocolate was warmed on a radiator. What would happen when you cooled down?*
▶ *You have a bar of chocolate. You want to make it into a chocolate egg for Easter. How would you do it? Why would it work?*
▶ *One really hot day, Penny came home from school with sticky, black tar from the road on her shoe. Her mum put the shoe in a plastic bag and left it in the freezer for a while. Afterwards, she was able to break off the black tar in pieces. Why did putting the shoe in the freezer make it easier to remove the tar?*

Permeability

What is permeability?
The *permeability* of a material is the rate at which it lets fluids, such as water, pass through it. A flour sieve is very permeable: water runs out of it as fast as it runs in. If you hold a large square of cotton fabric over a sink and pour water on it, the water builds up a little because the fabric is less permeable than the sieve. A large piece of blotting paper or kitchen paper is less permeable still. Porous materials often allow water a more or less free passage, according to the number and size of the pores. A sandy soil has large pores and an open structure. Rain permeates it quickly and passes through, so the soil is often dry. A sheet of plastic or foil has no pores, so these materials do not let water through: they are *impermeable*. A clay soil has few pores. Rain lies on its surface in pools and soaks away only slowly. Ponds in fields are lined with clay, so that the water stays on the surface.

Understanding permeability
Permeability can be confused with other words, such as *absorbency*. A kitchen towel can soak up and retain quite a lot of water, and so we say it is *absorbent*. It can also let water through, so it is also permeable. A sieve, however, is permeable but not absorbent. It does not soak up or retain water. The aim is to link permeability to the rate of flow of water, and not to the amount of water that the material soaks up and retains.

Steps to understanding
These steps establish the meaning of permeability and can also lay the foundation for learning about rocks and soils.

Age range and duration

The steps could be taken by most children, although you might want to limit the vocabulary to everyday terms with younger children. If you do all the steps on the same occasion and include some recording of what is learned, you will need to allow an hour for them.

Step 1: What material should we use for a hat on a rainy day?

You will need a few items to test with the children, such as a sieve, an old woollen garment, a cotton garment, cooking foil. You also need a jug, a dish of water and an empty dish to catch the water. Introduce the problem and ask the children to choose which they think would be the best material to use, justifying their choice. Test the materials in random order and use the outcome to put them in order from most to least permeable.

Talk: *What do we want a rain hat to do? Should water be able to get through it? Would this do? (Show sieve.) Why not? What about this? (Show another material.) Why do you think that? How could we test our materials? Let's see how fast water runs through them, using this jug. Let's start with the woollen sweater. Did it run through quickly? (Test the others and order them from most to least permeable.)*

Step 2: Why do some things let water through quickly?

Introduce the word *permeable*. Use the outcome of Step 1 and ask the children to speculate about why some materials are more permeable than others.

Talk: *Materials that let water through quickly are called 'permeable' materials. Which of these was the most permeable? Were there any that were not permeable? What do you think might make something permeable? (The sieve provides a clue, if one is needed.) So you think that more and bigger holes make things more permeable. How could we make the cooking foil permeable?*

Step 3: Check out your idea

You will need some magnifiers and the materials used in Step 1. With the children, look at how loose and open the fabrics are. Relate this to the observed permeability of the material. Ask the children to use their findings to suggest how they might make the cotton fabric more permeable (for example, perforate it using compasses). Test their suggestions.

Talk: *Have a look at the materials with the magnifiers. Can you see ways through it? Has it got tiny holes in it? What if we were to fold the sweater to make it really thick. Would that make a difference? Would it still be permeable? Could we make a folded, cotton blouse more permeable? How could we do that? Let's see if that works.*

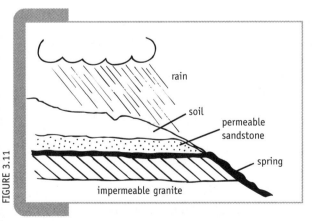

FIGURE 3.11

More to talk about and do

Springs, rivers and the water supply

Children are often surprised to find that some rocks, like sandstone, are permeable. Obviously, they are not as permeable as a thin layer of fabric, but water slowly passes through them. Explain the origin of springs. Impermeable rocks underneath the permeable ones stop the flow of water. The water builds up and may bubble out of a hillside as a spring (Figure 3.11).

FIGURE 3.12

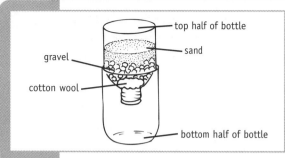
top half of bottle
sand
gravel
cotton wool
bottom half of bottle

Hands-on: filtering dirty water

Give the children a plastic pop bottle with the bottle top already cut off. Ask them to place a small piece of cotton wool loosely in the neck of the bottle. They should gently pour a layer of clean gravel on top of that. On top of that goes a thick layer of sand (Figure 3.12). How permeable is it? The children can check by gently pouring water onto the sand. (This will also wash out loose dust.) Next, the children should pour in some muddy water and wait. In time, cleaner water will come out the other end. This is a little like what happens to water as it soaks through the ground and rocks. Dirty water soaks down but it is filtered by the permeable rocks underneath. (None of the water should be tasted and the children should wear plastic gloves.)

Hands-on: absorbency and permeability compared

Ask the children to test a range of fabrics to see how much water each soaks up (absorbency). They can do this by marking the level of water in a dish, immersing the fabric, lifting it and holding it over the dish to let it drain, then marking the level of the water that is in the dish. The more the level goes down, the more absorbent the fabric must be. After this, they can test the fabrics to see how permeable they are by letting water run through them. Generally, permeability and absorbency increase as pores increase but only up to a point. After that, permeability continues to increase but absorbency falls off.

Checking for understanding

Check on the children's understanding with questions and tasks, such as:

▶ *Why are some coats better than others at keeping you dry?*
▶ *The people who make tea bags sometimes say that they 'let the flavour flood out'. What should a tea bag be like for this to be true? Why?*
▶ *A new paper towel soaks up a lot of water. Does this mean it will also let water run through it quickly?* (Yes/No/It depends.) *Tell me why you think that.*

Related topics
▶ Materials (page 89)
▶ Soils (page 96).

Soils

What is soil?

When rocks weather, they produce dust, sand, grit and gravel. Small plants and animals can live in this debris. In time, the plants and animals darken it with their own organic matter. The mix of debris and organic matter is what we call a *soil*. One half of a good soil is rock debris with a dash of organic matter. The rest comprises equal amounts of air and water. Debris from different rocks, sorted differently by wind and water, can produce different soils. Soils are very important because they often support life. They provides nutrients, water and somewhere for plants to anchor themselves. Without the plants that soils support, animal life as we know it would have a hard time. Soils are also habitats for a variety of animals, useful building materials for earthworks like embankments, and filters and storage for the water we drink.

Understanding soils

As with most commonplace materials, everyone thinks they know what soil is. They are so familiar with it that its variety and importance are overlooked. For children, a soil is for play, it may be a source of germs, grass grows on it, it is generally less painful to fall on than concrete, and it results in dirty hands, dirty clothes and annoyed parents. The aim is to help them notice its variety and understand that soils do important things for us and other animals.

Steps to understanding

The first few steps apply the senses to soils. You will need three or four different soils for the children to examine. Collect samples from different places so that you have different colours and textures. Such soils will also probably have different compositions. If the children are to handle the soils, ensure that they wear plastic gloves or plastic bags over their hands.

Age range and duration

Most children could learn something from these steps, regardless of age. Allow an hour to complete the steps, putting aside time for other activities and written work that you may include. If you include your favourite soil activities and some written work, you may prefer to take Step 1 on one occasion and the remaining steps on another. The extension ideas described after the steps would, of course, call for more time.

Step 1: Looking at soils

Place a teaspoon of each soil on squares of white paper. Ask the children to describe how the soils are similar and how they are different. Wearing a plastic glove, take a pinch of each soil and smear it on white paper. This can emphasise and draw attention to colour differences. Have the children examine the soils with a magnifier. Allow them to probe and sort the soils a little using tweezers. The aim is to see if they differ in composition.

> **Talk:** (Show the first sample.) *Do you know what this is? Here's some more. (Show other samples.) Are they the same? Tell me some ways that they are the same. What's different about them? Watch, I'm going to smear them out on paper. Are they all the same colour? Do you think they all came from the same place? Are soils in different places the same? Let's look more closely: use the magnifiers. Try sorting out each soil. What is that stringy bit? Is it a dead root? Are there any tiny stones … grit. Which soil has the most grit? Which has the biggest bits of grit?*

Step 2: Smelling soils

Damp soils often have distinctive smells. If the samples are dry, add a few drops of water to them and ask the children to sniff each in turn. The aim is to see if the soils can be distinguished by smell.

> **Talk:** *Do they all smell the same? What do the smells remind you of?*

Step 3: Listening to soils

If there is grit or sand in a soil, it can make a scratching noise when smeared on paper. Clay soils, on the other hand, contain a lot of very fine particles and these spread out smoothly and quietly. Ask the children to smear a pinch of damp soil on paper and listen to the noise it makes. Ensure they are wearing plastic gloves.

> **Talk:** *Do they sound the same? How are they different? What do you think makes that one scratchy? That sounds a good reason; how could we test it?* (A magnifier will often confirm differences in the amount and size of any grit in a soil.)

FIGURE 3.13

Step 4: Working soils

Soil scientists can distinguish between soils by their feel. They rub moist soils between finger and thumb, pushing them forward to make ribbons (Figure 3.13). A sandy, gritty soil makes only a short ribbon because it breaks up easily. A garden loam (with organic material in it) makes a longer, crumbly ribbon. A clay makes a long, sticky, shiny ribbon. Demonstrate it for the children. If they wear plastic gloves, you could ask them to try it for themselves.

Talk: *Are they all the same? How are they different? What do you think makes them different?*

More to talk about and do

The functions of soil

Discuss with the children what soils can do, for example:

▶ they provide plants with support so they do not fall over when it is breezy
▶ they provide plants with water
▶ they provide some of the other materials plants need, dissolved in the water
▶ they provide a home for animals (for example, moles, worms, centipedes and lots of microscopic animals)
▶ they can be used as building materials (for example, clay is used to make bricks)
▶ they behave like a sponge and soak up rainwater
▶ they filter the water that soaks through them.

Hands-on: sorting soils

A soil can be sorted into its constituents by adding it to water in a plastic bottle, shaking the bottle then leaving it to settle for a while. The heaviest materials sink first and form a layer. Lighter materials form layers on top of that. Organic material tends to float on the surface of the water. Different soils can be distinguished in this way.

Hands-on: some questions to investigate

Related topics
▶ Materials (page 89)
▶ Green plants (page 51)
▶ Permeability (page 94).

Ask the children one of these questions. Have them devise a way of investigating the problem.

1 *Is there air in soil?*
2 *Is there water in soil?*
3 *Is soil the same at different depths?*
4 *Do soils let water soak through easily?*

Checking for understanding

Check on the children's understanding with questions and tasks, such as:

▶ *One day you notice a sign that points left and says: To Redhills. There is another sign that points right and says: To Blacklands. When you look left, you see only green hills. When you look right, you see only green fields. How do you think these places got their names? How would you test your idea?*

▶ *Imagine you were marooned with a packet of melon seeds on a stony desert island. Could you make some soil so you could grow melons? What would you do?*

▶ *Suppose all the soil in the world blew away. Would it matter?*

Solids, liquids and gases

What are solids, liquids and gases?

Materials are generally a solid, a liquid or a gas at room temperature. They behave differently.

▶ Solids have a definite shape and a definite volume. A pencil sharpener is an example. Push it about a bit and it keeps its shape and has the same volume as before.

▶ Liquids have a definite volume but their shape can change. If you push a pool of coffee around on a table top, its shape changes but the volume of coffee stays the same.

▶ Gases do not have a definite shape or a definite volume. The air in a balloon is an example. It can be squeezed into another shape and even squeezed into a smaller volume. Some solids can be changed into liquids and then into gases by heating them. The heat breaks some of the bonds that hold the material together so the particles can move about more, either as a liquid or, with more heat, as a gas.

Understanding solids, liquids and gases

To children, the state of many materials is obvious. For example, a stone and a stick are solids (they are hard and keep their shape). Water and cooking oil are liquids (they are runny). These are useful starting points but leave a lot of materials in an ambiguous half world. For instance, 'Hard and keep their shape' could exclude a ball of wool. Since it is not runny, it cannot be a liquid either, so what is it? Again, the 'runny' idea is a useful starting point for distinguishing liquids as it captures the indefinite shape of a liquid. Children may not, however, appreciate its fixed volume (the classic, Piagetian conservation of volume problem). Recognising gases has its own difficulties in that they are often invisible. In addition, the word 'gas' in the UK can mean the fuel for central heating or an oven; in North America, it can mean the fuel for cars. The aim is to have children classify common materials as solids, liquids or gases and give good reasons for their classification.

Steps to understanding

Solids, liquids and gases are introduced as separate sub-topics. The steps use analogies and, to be successful, some time has to be given to making sure the children understand them. This is not a topic that has to be taught all at one sitting. Nor does it have to be taught only once. The foundations can be laid with young children and revisited and extended when they are older.

Age range and duration

With young children, you could spend a lot of time on the introductory steps of solids, liquids and gases. Older children are likely to benefit from revisiting some of the introductory experiences and then extending them with the remaining steps.

Solids

Step 1: An analogy for solids

Ask some children to behave like a rigid solid by forming a group held together by garden canes (or similar items; see Figure 3.14). As the group moves about, the children have no choice but to maintain their relative positions in it. This is the basis of the analogy for a solid.

FIGURE 3.14

Talk: *Is Jamie next to Grace? Who is next to David? Is Hayfa still next to Grace? Watch, they'll all move around but must keep a tight hold of the canes. Is Jamie next to Grace? Who is next to David? Is Hayfa still where she was? Has anything changed? Even though they've moved, everyone is still next to the same people.*

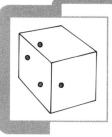

FIGURE 3.15

Step 2: Parts that stay in place

Have a large block of wood or a box to hand and a means of marking large, coloured dots on it (Figure 3.15). Begin by eliciting children's ideas about solids. Mark three or four large coloured dots on the box. Ask the children to tell you whether or not the dotted parts can move to somewhere else on the box. Relate it to the way Hayfa, Jamie, Grace and David maintained their places.

Talk: *Who can tell me what 'solid' means? Can you show me a solid? Show me another one. How do we know they are solids? Is this a solid?* (Show the block of wood.) *Watch, I'll put a red dot there, a blue dot there and a green dot there. If I leave it on the table, do you think the parts where the dots are will change place? If I throw it in the air and catch it, will the red dot place still be next to the blue dot place? Where will the green dot place be? What does this remind you of? Do you remember Hayfa, Jamie, Grace and David? What did they do? They were like something solid. They couldn't swap places. The bits in a solid are the same: they can't swap places.*

Step 3: Adapting the analogy for flexible solids

Some things we call solid are rather flexible, like an eraser. Ask the children to behave as in Step 1 but show that they can be squashed closer together without losing their places. Draw attention to the change in shape of the overall group. For instance, it can be squeezed to make it longer and thinner. This is a little like how a flexible solid behaves.

Talk: *What is different? Can we squash them together?* (Yes.) *This time, things are a bit looser, but are they still fastened to the same people?* (Yes.)

Step 4: Bendy, squashy and stretchy solids

Show several flexible solids, such as a jelly sweet, a marshmallow and an eraser. Illustrate their properties and discuss how they can behave like that.

Talk: *Is this solid?* (Holding up one of the items.) *Why do you think that? It's a bit squishy, isn't it? But do the bits lose their places? Let's try it.* (Put dots on the objects, as before. Gently flex them and squash them so that the children can see that the dots remain in the same place relative to one another.) *What does this remind you of?* (Relate it to the children's actions in Step 3 above.)

Liquids

Step 1: An analogy for liquids

Ask the children to behave like a liquid by forming pairs and trios held together by canes (Figure 3.16). As they move in a cluster, children in pairs and trios remain attached but the pairs and trios have more freedom to mix.

FIGURE 3.16

Talk: *Is Jamie still next to Grace? But what about Niaz, Peter and Amanda? They're still together but are they still next to Jamie and Grace? Is this like a solid? How is it different?*

Step 2: Parts that can change places

You will need a container of water and one of cooking oil. Begin by eliciting children's ideas about liquids and how they behave. Demonstrate the behaviour of liquids with the two examples of a liquid. Begin with the water, then show that the cooking oil behaves in the same way. For instance, you could introduce some glitter into the water and shake it vigorously to produce turbulent motion. This will show that the parts of water can move about much more freely than in a solid, even a flexible one. Relate the behaviour of liquids to the way the children were able to move in the analogy.

Talk: *Is water a solid? Why do you think it isn't a solid? Watch me shake it. What do you think is happening to all the bits of water? Are they keeping their places? Are they mixing up? What does it remind you of? How is it like when you were holding the sticks and moving about?*

Step 3: Distinguishing liquids and solids

Ask the children to distinguish some liquids from solids (such as, water, cooking oil, cod liver oil, treacle, PVA glue, orange juice, a piece of wood, a book, a piece of fabric, a ballpoint pen, a flower, a shoe). To finish, you could show a jelly, straight from the mould: is it a squishy solid or a thick liquid?

Talk: *Is this a solid or a liquid? Why do you think that?* (The jelly, if firm enough, is a flexible solid because its parts do not swap places, at least for the duration of the lesson.)

Gases

Step 1: The existence of air

Most common gases, including those in air, are invisible and some children may not believe that they exist, especially when they are still. This first step is to raise the children's awareness of air and then use that to illustrate the general properties of gases. Give the children a piece of stout card, 30cm or more square. Have them wave it in front of themselves to feel the resistance of the air. Also ask the children to 'scoop' air with a plastic beaker and release it under water to make it visible. You will also need a bucket of water, some plastic beakers and something to serve as lids or covers for the beakers.

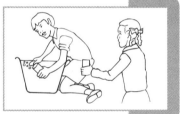

FIGURE 3.17

Talk: (Ask the children to wave their cards.) *What is it like? What can you feel? What makes that happen? Try it without the card. Make your hand like the piece of card. What does it feel like? What is it? Let's see if we can catch a cup of it.* (Ask the children to 'scoop' air with a plastic cup; see Figure 3.17.) *Cover the cup. Put it straight under the water. What's escaping? What was in the beaker? Where did it come from? Is it everywhere? Up in the corners of the room? Down on the floor? So air is everywhere, even though we can't see it. How does it get there? Can it move? What about when you walk through it? What must it be like?*

Step 2: An analogy for gases

You do not need canes for this analogy. Ask the children to move about singly and independently and fill the room. They should keep moving all the time and produce a continually changing random mix.

Talk: *Keep moving, everyone. I think this is a bit like what air does. Why do I think that? How is air different to a solid? How is it different to a liquid? Air is made of gases. This is how gases behave. Do you know any other gases? Can we pour them down the sink? Can we pack them neatly in boxes?*

Step 3: Gases move

Show that gases move about and can spread throughout a room. You may find it useful to have a taper or something similar so you can make a small amount of smoke. (Do not let the children handle the taper.) You will also need a drop or two of a strong perfume in a plastic bottle. Shake it to help it evaporate. This step makes further use of the analogy.

Talk: *Gases, like air, are a bit like smoke: they get everywhere. Watch.* (Demonstrate the behaviour of a little smoke. Point out that the smoke is still able to move around even though the room is full of air. You could simulate this using a large number of children as the air and a small number of children carrying SMOKE labels as the smoke. The latter have to mix with and spread out through the larger number of 'air' children.) *Look at this bottle. It looks empty. Is there anything in it? What will happen if I take the top off? Why do you think that? Let's find out. Can you see anything happening? No, we can't. I can tell something is coming out. Do you know how I can tell something's coming out? Can you tell something is coming out? So, what was in here is spreading out everywhere. That's what gases do.*

More to talk about and do
Air
There are not many gases the children can work with. Therefore, supplement their practical work with further talk. For example, air is a mixture of gases (mainly nitrogen and oxygen, with a dash of carbon dioxide). Smoke adds other gases to it as well as small particles. It is the particles that make smoke visible. Other gases children may have heard of are hydrogen and helium in balloons. Fog comprises tiny droplets of water suspended in the air and it behaves like a gas in some ways. What we see above a cup of hot liquid, or coming from a kettle, is actually a fog-like vapour. True steam is another invisible gas and needs to be above about 100°C to stay like that.

Related topics
▶ Materials (page 89)
▶ Changes (page 80)
▶ Evaporation (page 86)
▶ Melting (page 92).

Hands-on: watching ice melt
Children should observe and record ice melting to produce water, although heating water to make steam is too hazardous for them.

Checking for understanding
Check on the children's understanding with questions and tasks, such as:
▶ *Look at this ball. Is it a solid, a liquid or a gas? Why do you think it is a solid?*
▶ *Look at this soap* (show a sample of liquid soap). *Is it a solid, a liquid or a gas? What makes you think it is a solid?*
▶ *When you slice onions, it can make your eyes water. If you slice them in a dish of water, it doesn't do that. Why not?*

Stretching
• •

What is stretching?
Stretching is when the length of something increases as it is pulled. A spring is an obvious example, but all solids will stretch to some extent although it may be only by a microscopic amount. There are two important things to look for.
▶ The first is whether or not the object returns to its original shape when released. If it does, we say it is *elastic*.
▶ The second is that there can be a pattern to stretching. With some things, if you double the pull, you double the amount it stretches; three times the pull gives three times the stretch, and so on. Springs will often behave like this, as can a thick elastic band, to some

extent. Other materials do not follow this pattern. Some plastic bags, for instance, stretch very little to begin with, then stretch a lot when the contents are heavy.

All materials reach the point where their springiness goes haywire and they stretch uncontrollably or snap. A spring, for example, can be pulled to the point where it will not return to its original shape. In other words, it is no longer elastic. Plastic bags can behave the same after they have been overloaded.

Understanding stretching

The first problem is that this topic can seem pointless. Why is knowing how things stretch worthwhile? Who cares? Children also tend to concern themselves unduly with the breaking point of things rather than with what happens before that. The term *elastic* is also often used as a synonym for a rubber band. The aim is to help children see the relevance of the topic, grasp the meaning of *elastic* and learn how materials might respond to stretching forces.

Steps to understanding

This path to understanding begins with the relevance of the topic. The second step establishes the meaning of the word *elastic*. The final step looks for patterns in stretching.

Age range and duration

The first two steps can be introduced at an early age. Older children will need the final step, but they still need to be reminded of the topic's relevance and the meaning of *elastic*. If you are working with younger children and are taking only the first two steps, you will need an hour or so, not including time for written or other activities. Older children should also take these steps but will need less time. The time needed for the remaining step depends on how many items you include for testing. With some written work, it could easily take another hour.

Step 1: Why are we doing this?

This step aims to make explicit some reasons for learning about stretching things. It draws attention to practical applications of elastic materials. You need a few examples, such as: the elastic webbing under the cushion of a seat (you may have such a chair in the staff room), an item of clothing made with an elasticated fabric, such as Lycra®, a buggy propelled by an elastic band.

> **Talk:** *What makes a chair comfortable? What about this chair? What does this do? (Draw attention to the webbing.) What about this sweater? If I stretch it, do I want it to stay stretched? What helps to keep it in shape? Look at the label. Can you see something else in the classroom that is meant to stretch and go back into shape? Do you know of something else like that at home? So, are stretchy things useful? Invent me a use for something stretchy. Draw a picture of it for everyone to see.*

Step 2: The meaning of *elastic*

This is essentially a sorting activity. You need a number of items to test, such as: a length of garter elastic, arm bands to hold up shirt sleeves, a length of thick string, a bath sponge, a strip of carpet, a safe (perforated) plastic carrier bag, a piece of felt, a cotton

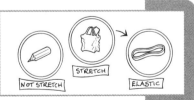

FIGURE 3.18

shirt sleeve, a length of wood, a sausage-shaped piece of modelling clay. You also need hoops to group the sorted items. Th first sort divides the items into things that stretch noticeably and things that do not. The second takes the 'stretch' group and sorts out the 'elastic' items (Figure 3.18). See also Photocopiable Thinksheet 26 on page 111.

Talk: *Is this stretchy? Can we see it stretch? Yes, so let's put it into this hoop. What about this? No, I can't see it stretching so where should I put it? (and so on) Look at all the things in this hoop (STRETCH). These all stretched. Let's try them again. Watch carefully. See it stretch? What happens when I let go? Does it go back to what it was? How can we be sure? Let's draw around it before we stretch it. Now, let's stretch it and see if it goes back to what it was. When something goes back to its starting shape, like this, we call it 'elastic'.*

Step 3: How much do things stretch?

In this step, the effect of steadily increasing the pull on various objects is noted. This can be done in different ways according to the age and experience of the children. For younger children, hang a plastic carrier bag on a chair and add similar cans of food to the bag,

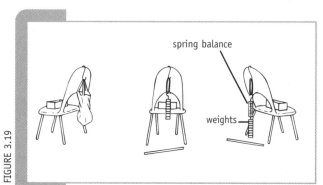

FIGURE 3.19

measuring how much it changes in length each time a can is added. Test a paper carrier bag and one made from a more elastic fabric in a similar way and compare. (Take care to put something on the chair so that the loaded bags do not make it topple.) Another way is to ask older children to measure various items (like a rubber band, a length of cotton cloth, a leg from a pair of tights) when countable, equal weights are added to them. A third way is to test equal strips of various materials using a force meter. In all cases, ensure that the supports for the materials and objects are secure and that nothing can fall on the children. It usually helps if the children work on the floor. Figure 3.19 shows the alternative approaches.

Talk: *How much did it stretch? Hang on another one. How much more did it stretch? Is that more than last time? Is it about the same? Is it less? How much more do you think it will stretch if you hang another one on? Try it and see if you are right.*

More to talk about and do

Squashing

Materials, like sponge seats and bed springs, can be squashed. The amount they squash depends on how hard you push. With some materials, if you double the push, you double the amount of squash. Talk about and explore this aspect with the children, establishing its relevance and the meaning of *elastic* in this context.

Hands-on: squashing things

Having tried stretching things, the children have the basis for testing things that can be squashed. Items you might include are: a sponge, a pile of paper, a pile of fabrics such as felt, and a block of clay. Of these, the sponge should be fairly elastic. Do remember to ensure that heavier objects are secure and that children work safely.

Checking for understanding

Related topics
- Materials (page 89)
- Changes (page 80)
- Forces (page 124).

Check on the children's understanding with questions and tasks, such as:
- (Show some object that can be stretched. Demonstrate it.) *Is it stretchy? Is it elastic? Why do you think that?*
- *Why is being stretchy helpful to us? If the seat of this chair was not stretchy, what difference would it make? If it was not elastic, what difference would it make?*
- *What would the ideal carrier bag be like? Why would that make it ideal?*

Changes

Match up the changes

The pictures show things before and after they have changed.

1 Draw lines to join the 'befores' with the 'afters'.
2 Were these fast changes, slow changes or very slow changes? Write on each line how fast the change would be.
The first one has been done for you.

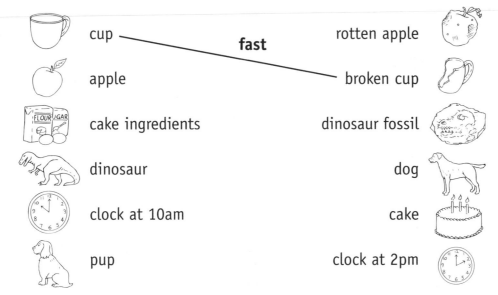

Filling in the gaps

These pictures show some changes.
The first picture shows what it was like to start with.
The last picture shows what it was like after it changed.

In the boxes in the middle, draw what they looked like in between.
The first one has been done for you.

Worzel or not Worzel?

This is Worzel, the timid scarecrow. If he only changes his clothes, he is still Worzel. But if he changes his head, he becomes a new person.

1 Pick out changes that leave Worzel the same person and write WORZEL under them.

2 Pick out the ones that make him different and give them new names.

WORZEL

3 Draw two scarecrows yourself. The first one should be a Worzel that is not like any of the ones above but is still Worzel. The second one should be a different-person Worzel who is not like any of those above.

Your Worzel	Your different-person Worzel

Chemical changes (sidebar)

Dissolving around us

Which picture shows something dissolving or about to be dissolved?

Which sweet lasts longest?

You are given a mixture of sweets and can have one to suck on the way to school. You want a sweet that will last as long as possible. The problem is, which one?

Invent an experiment that will test the sweets to find out which one will last longest. Remember, it must be a fair test. Write a plan for the experiment on another sheet of paper. Your plan must include:

a) what you want to find out
b) what you will do (draw a picture to show this)
c) how you will set out your results
d) how you will know which sweet is the one to suck on the way to school.

Dissolving

Evaporation

Will a big pool dry up faster than a small pool?

This was Elsa's experiment. She started it well. Elsa made pools of water on three plastic plates. She used the straw and put one drop on one plate to make the smallest pool. Then she used the straw to put another drop on another plate. She spread it out to make a bigger pool. Then she put another drop on the last plate and spread it out to make the biggest pool. So she had a small pool, a medium pool and a large pool. Elsa waited a minute or two but nothing seemed to happen. She was sure that the small pool should evaporate first, so she blew at it for a while. That seemed to help. Next, she stood it on the window ledge while she had a look at the

others. "Good," she thought. "The big pool is still there." She poked it around for a while, then put it next to the sink in case it made a mess. She glanced at the medium pool and decided it would be safe enough on her table.

1 Was this a good experiment?
2 Why do you think that?
3 What would you do?

Does warm water evaporate faster than cold water?

This was Warren's experiment. He put a drop of water in the middle of a plate and stood the plate over a hot radiator. He watched it closely and saw that it disappeared after about three minutes. "Wow!" he thought. "Warm water does evaporate faster than cold water."

1 Warren could be right, but was this a good experiment?
2 Why do you think that?
3 What would you do?

Making groups

1 Can you group the things in the picture? What is the same in each group?

2 Next, try to group the things in the picture a different way.

3 What is the same in each group this time?

Melting

Nasir's experiment

One snowy day, everyone made snowballs in the school playground. Nasir brought the snowballs he had made into the classroom. He asked Miss Hayes if he could keep them for later.

"There'll be nothing left for later!" Miss Hayes said.

"Why?" asked Nasir, disappointed.

"Let's find out," said Miss Hayes.

This is what they did:

Miss Hayes put each snowball into a plastic cup.

She put a cup with its snowball on the windowsill where it was cold.

She put a cup with its snowball on Nasir's table where it was warm.

She put a cup with its snowball on the radiator where it was hot.

She wrapped a scarf around a cup with its snowball and stood it next to the one on Nasir's table.

At the end of the lesson, everyone went to see the snowballs. This is what they found:

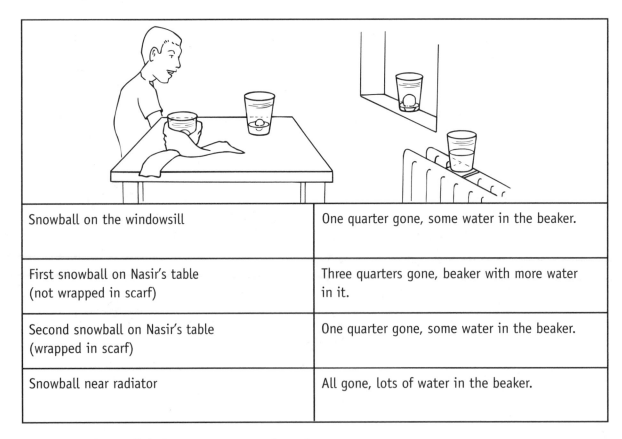

Snowball on the windowsill	One quarter gone, some water in the beaker.
First snowball on Nasir's table (not wrapped in scarf)	Three quarters gone, beaker with more water in it.
Second snowball on Nasir's table (wrapped in scarf)	One quarter gone, some water in the beaker.
Snowball near radiator	All gone, lots of water in the beaker.

1 **Where did the water come from?**

2 **Why was it different for the different snowballs?**

3 **What did this experiment show about scarves?**

Things that can stretch

Some of these pictures show things that can stretch.

1 How many stretchy things can you find? Colour the ones you find. Leave the others uncoloured.

If something is elastic, it goes back to the shape it was to start with when you stop stretching or squashing it.

2 How many of your stretchy things do you think are elastic? Put a tick next to the ones you think are elastic.

Stretching

chewing gum	eraser	modelling clay	jelly baby
telephone cable	rope	catapult	brick
shoe	sock	paper	pencil
bread	balloon	flower	chain necklace
can of food	coin	bendy straw	marshmallow

Chapter 4
Physical processes

This chapter gives you ways of helping children grasp various physical processes that have to do with forces, motion, light, sound, magnetism and electricity. These physical processes are often invisible. For instance, we cannot see the force of gravity, the force of a magnet, an electrical current in a wire or sound travelling across a room. What we can see are their effects, and from these we infer their causes. It helps children to understand if you make the invisible visible, even if only through simple analogies.

The topics in this chapter are organised alphabetically in order to make it easy to locate the one you want. Use them to support your normal routine when teaching science. Dip into them as you need. The table below shows when the topics are likely to be useful.

Topic	When to use the topic
Echoes	▶ when explaining how sound travels through materials like air ▶ when investigating and explaining properties of sound.
Electrical circuits	▶ when explaining simple series circuits using various components, such as switches ▶ when teaching children how to draw circuits.
Energy	▶ when introducing the concept of energy ▶ when distinguishing between mechanical energy and force ▶ when investigating how far buggies will go.
Floating and sinking	▶ when explaining the properties of materials and objects in water ▶ when exploring different kinds of force ▶ when investigating what makes things float.
Forces	▶ when introducing the concept of a force ▶ when investigating the effects of a force ▶ when laying the foundations for measuring forces.
Friction	▶ when teaching about different kinds of natural forces ▶ when explaining friction between solids ▶ when explaining friction in air and water ▶ when investigating friction as a force opposing motion.
Gravity	▶ when introducing the concept of gravity as a downward pull of the Earth on things ▶ when investigating what gravity can do.
Light sources	▶ when introducing the concepts of light, light sources and light reflectors ▶ when investigating reflection from different surfaces.
Magnetism	▶ when introducing the concept of magnetism ▶ when teaching about the properties and uses of magnetism.
Mirrors	▶ when explaining the regular reflection of light from a mirror ▶ when investigating the way light reflects from a mirror.
Shadows	▶ when exploring the properties of light ▶ when explaining why there are shadows ▶ when explaining the size of shadows ▶ when teaching that light travels in straight lines.
Sound	▶ when teaching about the cause of sound ▶ when explaining differences in loudness and pitch ▶ when investigating the relationship between the properties of an object and the sound it makes.

Echoes

What are echoes?

Imagine you throw a pebble into a pool of water. It makes a water wave that moves out in all directions until it hits something. Sound behaves in the same way. If you shout, sound spreads out through the air until it hits something. When it hits something, it bounces back, just like the water wave. You hear your own shout and then you hear the one that bounces back – the echo. Why do we not hear echoes bouncing off the walls around us? Sound moves quickly (it covers about 330 metres in each second), so the time between a sound and its echo in a classroom is only a fraction of a second. That makes it hard to notice. You notice echoes more when you are a long way from a wall or cliff so that the sound takes a second or two to get there, bounce off and return to you. In very large rooms, sound can bounce from wall to wall. These reverberations add to the original sounds and can make them indistinct. Great care is needed when designing concert halls if these echoes are not to spoil the music.

Understanding echoes

Sound is invisible, which is probably just as well, given the sea of noise we live in. But it also means that children cannot see what happens as it spreads out and bounces from things. The aim is to give the children something to think with to help them grasp how sound behaves in air.

Steps to understanding

- Step 1 introduces the problem.
- Step 2 provides a concrete analogy for sound travelling through air.
- Step 3 uses the analogy to explain the existence of echoes.
- Step 4 explains why echoes are generally not noticeable in or near buildings.

Age range and duration

The first three steps are appropriate for all but the youngest children. You may want to keep the final step for older children. Together, you should allow at least half an hour for the steps, putting aside the time you might want to give to written or additional activities.

Step 1: Noticing echoes

Stand the children some distance from a large wall (for example, about 100 metres away from the school wall or from a large building facing the school). Ask them to stand quietly while you clap your hands. (If the echo is faint, you can use two dustbin lids like cymbals to make a louder sound. A short blast on a whistle can work well, too.) Make sure that the children know that the noise from the wall is called an *echo* and have them try to explain it. This sets the scene and the problem: how do we explain echoes? You could conclude by asking the children to take turns to make an echo themselves.

> **Talk:** *Listen! Can you hear it? What is it? Where does the echo come from? What makes the echo? Tell me what you think happens.*

Step 2: An analogy for the way sound travels through the air

You need a toy slinky spring. If possible, choose a long, metal one. If the children are not familiar with a slinky spring, let them explore its properties, particularly its 'springiness'. Stretch it along a smooth table. Hold one end while a child holds the other (Figure 4.1). Push forward quickly and send a pulse along the spring. It will travel towards the other end. At this stage, do not attempt vigorous pulses, simply let the children see the pulse and how it moves away from you. Tell them that this is how sound moves through the air from one person to another. The air behaves like a spring. To emphasise it, give a shout as you send a pulse out.

FIGURE 4.1

sound

Talk: *Watch! I'm going to give a quick push. There! Did you see it? I'll do it again. That's a bit like how noises move through the air. The air is a bit like a spring, just like our slinky spring. When you shout, the sound moves through the air and reaches someone's ears. Watch. Hoi! See it move out towards Oliver?*

Step 3: Using the analogy to explain echoes

Remind the children of the sound echoes that they heard. In this step, you relate sound echoes to the analogy. With the spring as in Step 2, send a vigorous pulse along it as you shout. The child holding the other end of the spring is like a wall. The pulse will bounce from that end and come back to you. If necessary, draw the children's attention to it. Have them relate the bouncing back effect to the way sound bounced off the wall.

Talk: *When we were outside, what did we hear? Do you think we can make echoes with our spring? How might we do it? Let's give it a try. Watch! Did you see it bounce back from Oliver? How is that like the echoes we heard? We can't see a sound but, if we could, we would see it bounce off the wall just like this.*

Step 4: Explaining why the classroom is not full of echoes

Since we know that sound bounces off things, why is the classroom not full of echoes? Use the spring as in Step 3. Send a vigorous pulse along the spring and ask the children to notice the time between when you send it and when it returns. Use a much shorter length of the spring by having a child grip the spring as in Figure 4.2. Repeat the vigorous pulse. It will return relatively quickly. Relate this to the nearness of the walls in the classroom. They are very close and the sound bounces back to us so quickly that we cannot separate the echo from the original sound. There is next to no time between the shout and its echo so we do not notice it.

FIGURE 4.2

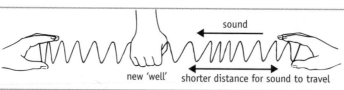

new 'well' shorter distance for sound to travel sound

Talk: *What do sounds bounce off? The classroom has walls; why don't we hear echoes all the time? What's the difference? These walls are closer. How will that make a difference? Let's give it a try with our slinky spring. See how long it takes for a 'shout' to go from me to Oliver and back again. Hoi! Now let's bring the wall closer. Hoi! Was there a difference? I'd hardly shouted before the echo came back. There was next to no time between my shout and the echo. So, in the classroom, why do we not hear the echoes?*

More to talk about and do

Bats finding their way in the dark

Ask the children to find out and talk about how bats use high-pitched squeaks to find their way in the dark.

Hands-on: investigating with the slinky spring

To be meaningful, an analogy has to be familiar. Give the children some time with the slinky spring to learn about its properties. Let them try sending 'sounds' through it so that they echo. Ask them to investigate for themselves how the time between the sound and the return of the echo depends on the distance. To do this, two children stretch the spring along a smooth table. A third child takes the part of the wall. He or she grips the spring at different points to make the 'sound' bounce back (as in Figure 4.2). The children will find that the time decreases as the distance to the 'wall' decreases.

Checking for understanding

Check on the children's understanding with questions and tasks such as:

▶ *Do you think there would be echoes in big rooms? Why?*
▶ *If you stand among several big buildings, you can sometimes hear lots of echoes if the buildings are not too close. Why?*
▶ *When submarines are under water, they send out pinging noises and listen for echoes. How does this help them? How does it work?*
(See also Photocopiable Thinksheet 27 on page 144.)

> **Related topics**
> ▶ Sound (page 141).

Electrical circuits

What is an electrical circuit?

An electrical circuit has to be complete if it is to work. Suppose you have a torch bulb connected to a battery (Figure 4.3). The battery makes the bits of electrical current energetic. They flow from the battery to the bulb. In the bulb, they pass on some of their energy to the filament. This makes the filament very hot and it glows. If the electricity had nowhere to go, no more electricity could get into the bulb so the bulb would cool and go out. The problem is solved by giving the electricity a way back to the battery. This lets the electricity flow from the battery, around the loop and back to the battery for recycling. Now the bulb glows continuously because electricity flows though it continuously. It is the same for other electrical components and devices. Buzzers and electric motors, food mixers and televisions all need complete circuits to make them work.

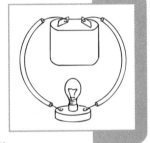

FIGURE 4.3

Understanding an electrical circuit

Children may think that electricity flows from the battery to the bulb where it is consumed as it makes the bulb glow. For these children, the other wire that goes back to the battery is not needed. This is not entirely unreasonable – after all, petrol is consumed in a car so why not electricity in a light bulb? The aim is to help the children shed this 'fuel' view of electricity and grasp the need for a complete circuit.

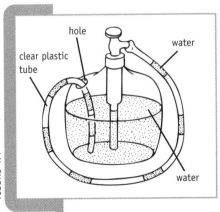

FIGURE 4.4

Steps to understanding

An analogy can help children understand electrical circuits better. The one here draws parallels between water flow and electricity flow. You will need an empty, pump-action soap dispenser and a length of clear, flexible tube that will fit over the spout of the dispenser. With due care, carefully cut a hole in the shoulder of the dispenser to take the other end of the tube. Half fill the dispenser with water. A few drops of food colouring make it more visible. When the top is pressed, water will flow through the tube and back into the dispenser (see Figure 4.4).

Age range and duration

Analogies work only when they mean something to the children. Steps 1 and 2 are to make sure of that. Allow about fifteen minutes for these (older children may not need that). Allow a further hour for Steps 3 and 4. You may prefer to leave Steps 5 and 6 for another occasion and use them to extend and consolidate learning. They need about 30 minutes. The analogy has been found to be effective with children as young as seven years of age (see also Introduction). It probably has increasing potential from this age upwards.

FIGURE 4.5

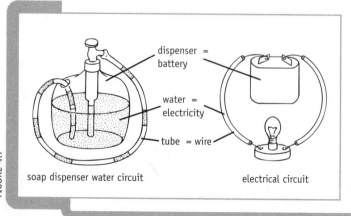

Step 1: Water running through a tube

Show how water runs through a pipe as it is poured through a funnel into a transparent tube and then into a dish (Figure 4.5).

Talk: *What happens to the water? Where does it go? If I pour all the water in this jug in at this end, how much comes out the other end? How can we check that idea? What goes in must come out.*

Step 2: Pumping water through a tube

Now squeeze water from a washing-up liquid bottle through the tube to introduce the idea of a pump. Attach another washing-up liquid bottle to the other end of the tube. Ask the children to predict which way the water will go when both bottles are gently squeezed (Figure 4.6). (Do not overdo the squeeze if you do not want to be sprayed with water!)

FIGURE 4.6

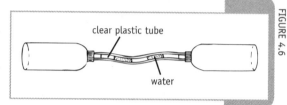

clear plastic tube

water

Talk: *Which way will the water go? Why won't the water flow when we squeeze both bottles at the same time? What will happen if I squeeze one bottle harder than the other?*

Step 3: The electrical circuit

Set out a battery, a torch bulb in a holder and some wires. Ask the children to tell you how they think you might make the light bulb come on. Try their ideas and explore their thinking. Set up a circuit like the one shown in Figure 4.3 so that the bulb is on. Invite the children to explain how it works and, in particular, why a return wire to the battery is needed.

Talk: *What are these? What could I do with them? How would I do that? Where does this bit go? Will that make the bulb light up? Why do you think that? (When you have reached a working circuit, or constructed it yourself, follow in a similar vein.) Why does this work? Will it still work if I take this wire away? Look, the bulb has gone out. Why does this wire have to be there?*

FIGURE 4.7

dispenser = battery

water = electricity

tube = wire

soap dispenser water circuit

electrical circuit

Step 4: Supporting understanding with the water circuit analogy

Show the soap dispenser and ask what it does. Show it pumping water. Fit a tube and pump water around the water circuit. (Food colouring or ink in the water will make it more visible.) Put your soap dispenser water circuit next to an electrical circuit and match them: pump and battery, tube and wire (see Figure 4.7).

Talk: *Can we see electricity? It's invisible, isn't it? As it's invisible, we can imagine that it does what the water does. Why do we need that wire, the one from the bulb and back to the battery?*

Step 5: Applying the water circuit analogy

You will need the circuit in Figure 4.3 and an extra battery. The water circuit can be used to make some predictions about electrical circuits. In this case, the idea is to use the water circuit to predict what will happen when you use two batteries in the electrical circuit.

Talk: *Suppose we had two batteries and joined them up like this* (pointing at each other); *what difference would it make? Why do you think that? Let's think it through. If we had two pumps pointing at each other, what would happen? The water would not move. What does that tell us about what the electricity will do? And what does that tell us about the bulb? Suppose we put the two batteries pointing the same way. What difference would that make? Why do you think that?*

Step 6: Some differences

A water circuit can help us understand an electrical circuit, but no analogy is perfect. Illustrate this by taking the tube out of the dispenser so that water runs out as the dispenser is pressed. Electricity does not run out of a wire like this. Ask the children to think of other differences. For example, battery electricity is invisible but water is not.

Talk: *What will happen when I cut this wire? Will electricity run out all over the place? Does a water circuit always do the same thing as an electrical circuit? Can you think of other ways that they are different?*

More to talk about and do
The dangers of high voltage electricity

Normally, an electrical current is confined to the wires. It does not run out like water from a burst pipe. High voltage electricity, however, can be so energetic that it can jump from a wire across a gap. Pylons carry high voltage electricity high above the ground for that reason. If you climb a pylon, the electricity will take the easiest path it can. It will jump from the wires across to you and kill you. A lightning flash is made by high voltage electricity in clouds. When the invisible electricity jumps down, it heats the air and makes it glow along the path it took. That is what we call a *lightning flash*. Electricity from the mains supply in houses is powerful enough to kill if it passes through your body.

Hands-on: a pass-the-parcel analogy for electrical current

Another way of making the need for a complete circuit apparent is to use a pass-the-parcel activity. You will need lots of bulky parcels. The children sit in a circle. You feed in parcels and they pass the parcels around the circle. They have to keep them moving steadily. You now break the circle and the parcel current soon stops. You will need to point out that an electrical current is not exactly like this. The children should be able to suggest differences.

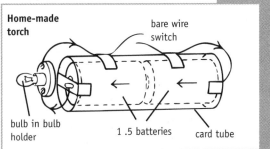

FIGURE 4.8

Hands-on: make a torch

Ask the children to make a torch from basic components (see Figure 4.8), such as a card tube, a battery, a bulb holder, a bulb and some wires. Afterwards, they should explain how the torch works, giving particular attention to the path of the electrical current. They can include a simple on–off switch and explain why that works, too.

Hands-on: conductors and insulators
Not everything lets electricity through as easily as a length of wire. Have the children test a variety of materials and classify them as conductors and insulators.

Checking for understanding
Check on the children's understanding with questions and tasks, such as:
▶ *Tell the story of a little bit of electricity as it travels around a circuit that has a battery and a light bulb in it.*
▶ *Ask the children to pretend that they have made a working electrical circuit with a battery, light bulb and a switch. Their friend is playing with the switch, pressing it so that the light bulb flashes on and off, over and over again. What will that be like for the little bits of electricity in the circuit?*

> ### Related topics
> ▶ Materials (page 89).

▶ *Show the children a copy of Photocopiable Thinksheet 28 (on page 145). Ask if the electrical circuit would work. Ask why it will not work. Ask how the children could make it work and have them explain their responses.*

Energy
. . . .

What is energy?
Imagine a wind-up car lying in the toy box. Before you wind it up, the spring inside is not able to turn the wheels and make the car move. When you wind it up, however, this coils the spring so it is ready to provide the force that turns the wheels. In science, this state of readiness of the spring is called *energy*. Scientists would simply say the tightly-coiled spring has energy. The energy of a wound-up spring, a stretched rubber band or a bent bow is called *mechanical energy*. There are other kinds of energy. The energy of fuels, food and batteries comes from the state of the chemicals in them, so it is called *chemical energy*. Heat, light, sound and electricity are forms of energy, too. If you know how to do it, one kind of energy can be changed into another. For example, the solar cell on a calculator changes light energy into electrical energy. You cannot, however, end up with more energy than you started. This is a scientific law known as the *conservation of energy*. (This should not be confused with conserving sources of energy, such as fossil fuels like coal and oil.)

Understanding the meaning of energy
Giving scientific meaning to the word *energy* takes care and time. First, the word is used in everyday language as though it were a substance. Breakfast cereals, glucose drinks and children, for instance, are often said to be full of energy. Children may already have acquired a 'substance' view of energy rather than a 'readiness' view. Children may also confuse energy and force. Energy itself is not a force, although it may be used to produce a force. The aim here is to give children something concrete to think about when considering energy.

Steps to understanding
When explaining energy, spring-driven toys with some of the mechanism visible give the children something concrete to think with. Each step takes the child into less obvious contexts. Use as many steps as meet your needs, but do not try to move on too quickly. Spread the steps over several lessons.

Age range and duration

Steps 1 and 2 (wind-up toys) go together and you should allow at least half an hour for them. Step 3 (gravity) could be taken on a different occasion, allowing about half an hour for it. Steps 4 and 5 (chemical energy) go together and could also be taken on a different occasion. Allow about three-quarters of an hour for these. These times exclude written and other practical activities you will want to include among the steps to consolidate the children's understanding. The first two steps can be taken by younger children. Older children could take all the steps.

Step 1: The state of the spring in a wind-up toy and what it can do

For this step, you will need a wind-up toy with a visible spring. Explore its action with the children and direct attention to the form of the spring when fully wound, partially wound and unwound. Relate that to what the vehicle can do.

Talk: *How do we make it work? Show me. What happens when you wind it up? When does it go a long way? What does the spring look like when it is ready to go a long way? What does it look like when it can't go far? And when it can't move at all?*

Step 2: Energy as 'something ready to change and do something for us'

Give each child a strip of fairly thick paper, about 2cm wide by 30cm long. Ask them to hold one end between the finger and thumb of one hand and then 'wind up' the strip to make a paper spring (Figure 4.9). Wound up like this, the spring is 'ready to change'. If we let it change, by releasing the outer end, it spins as it unwinds. This is what makes the wheels turn in the toy. In other words, we can get the wound-up spring to do something.

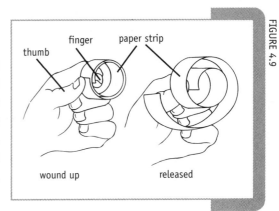

FIGURE 4.9

finger — paper strip — thumb

wound up — released

Talk: *Wind it up like this. Now, hold it. Do you think it's ready to change? How will we let it change? What will happen? Try it. See it spin? There's a spring in the toy car. Was it ready to change? What happened when it did change? Is the car's spring like our paper spring? Why do they not use paper springs in toy cars? Look at the car again. What's ready to change? If I let it change, can it do something for us? When there is something ready to change and do something, we say it has 'energy'. Has it got energy now? What about now (release the car so that it runs down)? If I had just come into the room and picked up the car, could I see if there was any energy left? How could I make a good guess about how much was left?*

Step 3: Gravity and energy

This step extends the concept to include *gravitational energy*. Hold an object in the palm of your hand at arm's length. Later, you will need a toy car connected by a thread to a small object that can pull it along on a table as the object falls (Figure 4.10).

FIGURE 4.10

Talk: *Is this ready to change? No? Well, watch. (Tilt your hand so the object falls to the floor.) Something changed, didn't it? What was it? So its height changed. Its height above the floor got less. In fact it hit the floor. Could we get that to do something for us? What could we get it to do? Look, we can make it move a toy car (Figure 4.10). So, there is something ready to change and it can do something as it changes. What do we say things like that have? Energy.*

Step 4: Chemical energy

This step extends the concept to *chemical energy*. You will need a battery-powered toy for this. Focus attention on 'something ready to change' (the chemicals in the battery). Remember not to let the children handle decaying or leaking batteries, and they should not use re-chargeable batteries. You will have safety regulations that cover the use of batteries and electricity in general.

> **Talk:** *How does this work? Does it have a spring? What makes it move? What's ready to change? But the battery looks just the same afterwards. Has it changed? How has it changed? It's changed inside. The materials inside it are different.*

Step 5: People power

Finally, extend the concept to include our own energy. What is it that is 'ready to change' inside us? (Food.)

> **Talk:** *Can you move a toy car? Of course, you can! But, you don't look like a spring. I think you're a bit like a battery. Why do I think that? What's ready to change inside you? (Food.) How's that a bit like a battery? (It has materials in it that change, although it does not look much different on the outside.) How do we know that the food changes inside us? What about this? (Show a foodstuff package.) It says it's full of energy. What does that really mean? Yes, it really means it's made of things that are ready to change inside us so we can do things.*

More to talk about and do

How much energy?

Energy is measured in *joules*, after the Victorian scientist, James Joule. One joule (1J) is roughly the energy needed to lift a cup of water from a table to your mouth. You may have to tell the children the convention that, even though it is a name, joule has a small letter at the beginning unless it is shortened to J. Ask the children to estimate how much energy is needed to do other simple tasks by comparing them with lifting a cup of water.

FIGURE 4.11

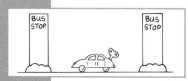

Hands-on: spring-powered toys

Explore the concept of energy as something ready to change. A coiled spring is 'ready to change' and so has energy available to make a toy move. Use a toy with a coiled spring (such as wind-up toy car – one where the spring is visible is very useful). Talk about a coiled spring as being ready to change and make the car wheels turn. Ask how far the car will go if the spring is wound up with only one turn of the key. Demonstrate the effect. How far will it go with two turns, three turns, etc? This activity allows you to develop the ideas in Steps 2 and 3. It is an opportunity to do some graph work relating the number of turns to the distance moved. After that, set up a pair of 'bus stops'. Ask the children to use their graphs to predict how many turns the spring will need to move from one bus stop to the next (Figure 4.11).

A useful way of rounding off this activity is to introduce a toy that works by compressing a spring (as in a pogo stick or a jumping bug). This time, the spring is not 'ready to change' when it is coiled up tightly. Instead, it is ready to change when it is squashed. Your conversation with the children about these toys is aimed at taking their thinking beyond spiral springs.

Hands-on: sand-powered toys

You can extend Step 3 by looking at the way that sand (or water) can fall and do something useful with its energy. There are sand-operated toys in which paddle wheels turn as sand

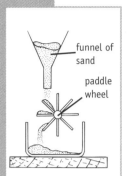

FIGURE 4.12

funnel of sand

paddle wheel

flows through them (Figure 4.12). This can also prepare children for a visit to a mill where a water wheel will let the children see a water-driven version on a bigger scale.

Checking for understanding

Check on the children's understanding with questions and tasks such as:
▶ (Stretch a large elastic band.) *Is there something ready to change here? What is it? Could we get it to do something useful?*
▶ *Tell me where this toy car gets its energy. Is there any energy ready now? How do you know?*
▶ *Think about a bow and arrow. Where does the arrow get its energy from?*
(See also Photocopiable Thinksheet 29 on page 146.)

Related topics
▶ Forces (page 124)
▶ Gravity (page 129)
▶ Electrical circuits (page 115).

Floating and sinking

Why do some things float and others sink?

If you put water in a dish, gravity pulls it down so it lies with a flat surface in the dish. If you put a block of wood in the water, gravity pulls that down, too. Some of the water is pushed aside (Figure 4.13). The water that is pushed aside presses down on the water below and makes the water below push up on the block. The upward push on the block is called the *upthrust*. If it is large enough, it will support the block (make it float). If it is not, the block will sink. You can feel the water's upthrust if you push down on the block of wood. The more you push down, the more water is pushed aside and the more upthrust there is. Suppose the block had been a brick. It would weigh much more than a wooden block of the same size. The upthrust would not be enough to keep it afloat.

FIGURE 4.13

block pushes water aside

water pushed aside, presses down on water below

water squeezed up, pushes up on block

But how can a steel ship float? A ship may be heavy but it is also big, because it is hollow. In fact, a ship is really quite light for its overall size (just imagine what it would weigh if it were solid). It makes a big dent in the water and pushes a lot of water aside. The upthrust can be big enough to match its weight. If the ship fills with water, however, the upthrust has to support the ship and the water in it. Usually, this is impossible and the ship sinks.

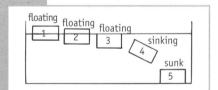

FIGURE 4.14

floating 1
floating 2
floating 3
sinking 4
sunk 5

Understanding floating and sinking

The children's thinking can present you with two problems. The first is what we mean by floating and sinking. Children tend to agree that something on its way to the bottom of a bucket is sinking and something that stays on the surface is floating. What about things that are partially submerged? For instance, a raft may float almost submerged. Children may be inclined to say that such objects (like number 3 in Figure 4.14) have sunk. In reality, they are floating. The children will need to know what counts as sinking and floating in science, otherwise you will not be talking about the same thing and explanations of floating and sinking will be ineffective.

The second problem is why some things float when others sink. What matters? Is it the size? Is it being hollow? Is it how heavy an object feels? Sometimes one rule seems to predict what happens and, at other times, another rule seems to work. Children have had several years of experience of things that float and sink, and will have acquired ideas that work in everyday life. For instance, they may know of two causes of flotation: being hollow and being lightweight. They use one or the other according to the situation. Take a ball. Is it hollow? If yes, then it will float. If it is not hollow, apply the alternative. Is it lightweight? If yes, then it will float. This works a lot of the time.

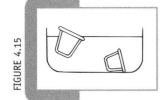

FIGURE 4.15

However, your aim is to move the children on the way to seeing a single cause of flotation – one that can explain why, for instance, one hollow jar floats when another one sinks, even though the jars weigh the same. The reason, of course, is that the first jar makes a bigger dent in the water, so is pushed up more (Figure 4.15).

Steps to understanding

The first step is to make sure that the children know what *floating* means in science. The other steps look at what makes things float.

Age range and duration

With younger children, you could focus on developing the meaning of *floating* (allowing half an hour or so for Steps 1 and 2). You could add the direct experience of *upthrust* and link it to why some things float (Steps 3 and 4, about half an hour). Finally, you could go further with older children and explain the source of upthrust and highlight the way bigger objects make bigger dents and bigger dents make more upthrust (Steps 5 and 6, allowing about 45 minutes). These times ignore the written and other tasks you are likely to include among the steps to consolidate learning.

Step 1: The meaning of floating

You need a range of objects, including some which float at different depths. Put them in a container of water for the children to see. Find out what the children mean by *float* and *sink* and, if necessary, tell them that barely, partly and almost completely submerged count as *floating*. Only things that end up on the bottom are said to have sunk. (There are very rare items that simply drift in the water, under the surface but not sinking to the bottom. Strictly speaking, these are neither floating nor sinking and are best avoided at this stage.) Afterwards, the children should test another collection of objects and classify them as floating or sinking themselves.

> **Talk:** *Has it sunk? Is it floating? What about this one? Look, this one is just floating. This one floats well; see how high it is in the water? This one is floating, too, but only just. That one's sunk to the bottom. What about this one? Is it floating or has it sunk to the bottom?*

Step 2: Feeling the upward push of the water

The aim in this step is to have the children feel the upthrust of water for themselves. Provide a block of polystyrene or a large, watertight, plastic ball and a bucket of water. Ask the children to push the item down in the water and feel the upward push of the water for themselves.

> **Talk:** *Push it down in the water. Does it go down by itself? What does it feel like? What is the water doing? Which way is the water's push? How might this make something float? Why do some things float very high in the water? Why do some things float low in the water? Why do some things sink?*

Step 3: Noticing the water that is pushed aside

This step is to draw attention to the water that is pushed aside when the block or ball dents the water in a bucket.

Talk: *Look at the water in the bucket. Clarissa, put your finger where the top of the water is. Keep it there. Watch what happens when Brendan pushes the block down. What happens? Why? How could you make the water level rise even more?*

Step 4: The pushed-aside-water pushes back

Why does the water push up on something? You need a plastic pop bottle with the bottom third cut off. Use the upper part of the bottle to 'dent' the water. With the bottle top on, the trapped air will dent the water. When you loosen the cap, the children will see the displaced water push water up inside the bottle. This is where the upward push comes from (Figure 4.16).

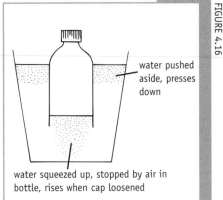

water pushed aside, presses down

water squeezed up, stopped by air in bottle, rises when cap loosened

FIGURE 4.16

Talk: *Look, I'm pushing down on the water. It's making a dent in the water. What has happened to the water that was in the dent? Where has it gone? Now I'm going to dent the water a different way. Can you see the dent? Can you see how the water level has risen around the bottle? Watch the water get pushed up to fill the dent. What makes it rise up like that? When you pushed the block down in the water, it made the water rise and you felt the water push up. What was making the water push up?*

Step 5: A big dent means a big upthrust

In an extension to the previous two steps, focus attention on the relationship between the size of the dent in the water and the upthrust. You need your bucket of water and the block of polystyrene or a ball.

Talk: *Let's try it again. Push the block into the water just a little. Has it dented the water much? How much is the water pushing up? Now push it in more. How much have you dented the water now? How much is the water pushing up? So, what can we say? The bigger the dent in the water, the more the water...?*

Step 6: Making reasonable predictions about what will float

Having found that big dents make more upthrust, the children should sort various items into those likely to make big dents (i.e. large items) and those that will not (i.e. small items). They should then consider each in turn. Given its weight and the amount it dents the water, will the upthrust be enough to keep it afloat?

Talk: *What about this one? Will it make a big dent? So, will it feel a large push up or a small one when it is in the water? Here, feel it. Is it heavy or light? Do you think the water's push will be enough to make it float? Let's try it.*

More to talk about and do

The skin on water

Still water behaves as though it has a thin, weak skin on the surface. Some insects are able to walk on this 'skin'. Books often have pictures of such insects and may show a sewing needle resting on the surface of water. This has nothing to do with why objects float or sink: that depends on the upthrust of the water. While water 'skin' effects are worth exploring, it is important that children do not confuse them with floating and sinking.

Hands-on: thinking about floating and sinking and testing ideas

What makes things float is not always easy for children to grasp because there are several things to think about at once. Keep a tray of everyday items and revisit the topic regularly. Ask the children to feel the weight of each item, consider the dent it will make and what that means for the upthrust. Then they should predict whether it will float or sink (see also Photocopiable Thinksheet 30 on page 147).

Hands-on: explaining the unexpected

Collect a few items that behave unexpectedly in water. These make good puzzles and science conversation starters. Find two empty jars, one of which floats while the other sinks (this means that the first must make a bigger dent in the water and so feels more upthrust). You can also show the children a piece of pumice stone (you can obtain this from a pharmacy) and a pebble of the same size. Both dent the water about the same, but the pumice floats because it is light.

Checking for understanding

You could think in terms of three levels of understanding. First, there is the meaning of the word *floating*, then there is *upthrust*, and then there is the relationship between the dent and the upthrust. Not all of these may be appropriate for your children. The questions that follow are some examples that span this range of understandings.

▶ *Which of these is floating and which has sunk?* (See Photocopiable Thinksheet 30 on page 147.)

▶ *Why is upthrust called 'upthrust'?*

▶ *Why do some things float when others sink?*

Related topics
▶ Forces (page 124)
▶ Materials (page 89).

Forces

What is a force?

A force can change the shape of something, make things turn, change how something moves and change the direction of movement. The forces we make are generally of three kinds: pushes, pulls and twists. For example, when children squeeze a jelly sweet, stretch chewing gum, or twist a liquorice lace, they exert forces. The children push their thumb and finger together to squash the sweet, they pull on the gum to stretch it and they twist the lace as they turn it. If you push or pull a table, it moves away or comes towards you. Twisting, however, is different; it makes things turn. If something is already moving, a force can change how it moves. For example, if a child is cycling and puts his or her feet down, the cycle comes to a stop. (Even without feet on the ground, the cycle would stop if the child did not pedal because of the force of friction.) Another kind of change is when a force makes something change direction. A push from a gust of wind, for instance, may make the cycle change direction.

Understanding forces

A child has felt and used forces from (and even before) birth. For them, a push, pull or twist are rather mundane and they do not give them much attention. As a consequence, they may have acquired a concept of a force and know some of its properties but these may be largely unconscious. The aim is to provide a vocabulary, bring relevant prior knowledge into consciousness, and develop it.

Steps to understanding

These steps distinguish and label different kinds of force.

Age range and duration

They are suitable for children of all ages, although you may wish to omit the last step with the youngest children. Altogether, you should allow an hour for them. If you also ask the children to write about what you and they did, allow extra time for that.

Step 1: Pushes in the world

Illustrate some pushes by, for instance, pushing a large toy car along a table, pushing a drawer to close it, pushing a press-top pen. Tell the children these are pushes. Ask how many things they can see in the classroom that need pushes to make them work. Link 'push' to the word 'force'.

Talk: *What am I doing to the car? What am I doing to the drawer? I'm pushing it. Look, I'm pushing the pen top so I can use it. A push is a kind of force. Can you see anything else in the classroom that needs push forces to make it work? How many can you find? Which do you think needs the biggest push force? Which needs the smallest? Can we put them in order from biggest to smallest push force?*

Step 2: Pulls in the world

This step parallels Step 1. Illustrate some pulls by, for instance, pulling a large toy car by a string along a table and by pulling a cupboard door open. Tell the children these are pulls. Ask how many things they can see in the classroom that need pulls to make them work.

Talk: *What am I doing to the car? I'm pulling it. Look, I'm pulling the door open. A pull is another kind of force. Can you see anything else in the classroom that needs pull forces to make it work? How many can you find? Which do you think needs the biggest pull force? Which needs the smallest? Can we put them in order from biggest to smallest pull force?*

Step 3: Twists in the world

There may not be many examples of things that need twists in the classroom, so have a few ready (such as a pencil sharpener, plastic bottle with a screw top on, clock). Begin with a ball on a table and spin it between your finger and thumb. Proceed as in the previous steps.

Talk: *Am I pushing the ball? Am I pulling the ball? It's a bit of each, isn't it? It's making it spin. This is a twisting force. Can you see anything in the classroom that needs a twisting force? Can you think of anything at home that needs a twisting force (for example, a tap, a car's steering wheel)?*

More to talk about and do

Forces make things possible

Have a conversation with the children about the importance of forces. Are forces important in our lives? Do we use them a lot? Could we live without them? Think of the pushes, pulls and twists you do from the minute you get out of bed.

Hands-on: what can pushes, pulls and twists do to things?

Give the children some modelling clay and ask them to roll it into a fat cylinder. On the cylinder's side, ask them to mark a square with a pencil point (Figure 4.17). They should now draw

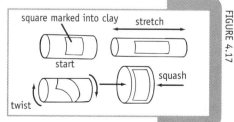

what it looks like. Ask them to predict what will happen to the shape of the square if they pull gently on the ends of the cylinder. Ask them why they think that. The children should now try it, then draw and explain what happens. Ask them to remake the cylinder, redraw the square and repeat the task but, on this occasion, they should push on the ends of the cylinder. Finally, ask them to try twisting the cylinder.

Hands-on: measuring forces
This would be a good time to introduce measuring pulls with a newton-meter. The unit of force is the *newton*. (Children will need to learn the convention: even though the unit is a name, it does not have a capital letter unless it is abbreviated. Scientists write: 5 newtons or 5N). The children can use the meter to test the order in which they placed pulls in the classroom in Step 2.

Checking for understanding
Check on the children's understanding with questions and tasks, such as:

▶ *Sort out the forces. Which are pushes and which are pulls?* (See Photocopiable Thinksheet 31 on page 148.)
▶ *This is a jelly baby. What will it look like if there are push and pull forces on it like the forces shown in the picture?* (See Photocopiable Thinksheet 31 on page 148.)
▶ *If there was no such thing as a force, what difference would it make? Why?*

Related topics
▶ Floating and sinking (page 121)
▶ Gravity (page 129)
▶ Magnetism (page 133).

Friction

What is friction?
Friction is a force that resists movement. For example, if you try to slide your hand across some sandpaper, you feel its rough surface holding you back. If you give a toy car a push along the floor, the car eventually stops moving because of friction between the wheels and the floor, and between the wheels and the axles. If you are cycling along a level road and stop pedalling, you eventually come to a stop for the same reason. Air and water will resist movement, too. Boats and aeroplanes are streamlined so that they slip through water and air more easily. This can reduce the amount of fuel they need for a journey. This makes it sound as though friction is always a nuisance, but it is not. For example, if there was no friction, nails would drop out of furniture, your shoes would not grip the floor, knives and forks would slip from your hands, and brakes would not work.

When you press the brake pedal of a car, friction between the brakes and parts of the spinning wheels brings the car to rest. What happens to all the energy that the car had? Energy cannot be lost, only changed from one form into another. In this case, the energy of the moving car becomes heat in the brakes. Sawing a piece of wood is another good example of the kind of change friction creates. There is a lot of friction between the saw teeth and the wood. Some of the energy of the moving saw cuts the wood, but friction changes some of it into heat, so the saw blade can become quite hot.

Understanding friction
Friction is a force we live with all our lives. For children, it can be a rather mundane matter of little consequence. They tend to notice friction more when it is at the extremes, as when it is small on ice or large in treacle. On other occasions, they may believe it is simply not there or is unimportant. The aim is to help children notice friction, grasp what it is and appreciate its role in our lives.

Steps to understanding

When direct experience is possible, it is hard to beat as support for understanding. These steps provide direct experience of friction and then go on to refine the concept.

Age range and duration

The first two steps are appropriate for all children while the last two suit all but the youngest. You should allow at least half an hour for the first two steps and a similar length of time for the other two steps. These times ignore the written and other tasks you are likely to include among the steps to consolidate learning.

Step 1: Feeling friction

Give the children the opportunity to feel friction for themselves. You need sheets of different papers. Their surfaces should vary in roughness from coarse and fine sandpapers, through emery paper, sugar paper, newsprint, to a glossy paper. Ask the children to feel the papers and describe them. Ask them to put them in order of roughness. Let the children push the papers over a board and feel the resistance to movement. Relate the roughness to the resistance. Check and develop the children's understanding of the word *friction*.

> **Talk:** *Do you think these sheets of paper will all feel the same? What will they feel like? Try them. What would you say this one feels like? Rough? Catchy? What about this one? Smooth? Slippery? Let's line them up. Put the roughest one here. Feel the others. Which should we put next? (Continue until you have a line of papers, sorted according to degree of roughness.) Watch. I'm going to turn the sandpaper over. Will it be hard or easy to push on the board? Why do you think that? Try it. Is it hard to push? What about this one? (Continue through the sequence to end with the glossy paper.) We say there is a lot of friction between the sandpaper and the board. What do you think that means? What would we say about the glossy paper? Does the friction pull forward or push back? Does it make it harder or easier to move things?*

Step 2: The cause of friction between solid surfaces

The children should now have an idea of the cause of friction. This step aims to make it explicit and reinforce it. You will need the papers used in Step 1 and some magnifiers. Ask the children to explain what causes friction and test their explanation by examining the different surfaces with the magnifiers.

> **Talk:** *Why is there more friction with sandpaper when it is moved on the board than with glossy paper? So you think that roughness is what matters? How could we check our idea? Let's check it with the magnifiers. What are we looking for?*

Step 3: When is friction a good thing?

Locate and have ready in your mind useful instances of friction in the classroom. For example, have a book and a pen with a grip pattern on it ready; have a shoe to hand to stand on a sloping board; note the spherical doorknob. Introduce these as talking points to clarify the focus of interest, then ask the children to think of other instances.

> **Talk:** *(Hold the book vertically between finger and thumb.) Look. Why doesn't the book slip through my fingers? Because it's rough? If I used the word 'friction', what would I say? There must be enough friction between my finger and thumb and the book to stop it slipping through. What about this shoe? Why doesn't it slide down the board? There must be enough friction between the shoe's sole and the board to keep it in place. What about the doorknob? If there was no friction between my hand and*

the doorknob, what would happen? Would I be able to open the door? (Continue like this until you are satisfied that the children see that instances of useful friction could be all around them.) Now I want you to look around and find somewhere different where friction is useful.

Step 4: When is friction a bad thing?

You will need a toy car, a clear table-top, a small quantity of cold cooking oil and some paper towels. Use the car and table-top to remind the children that a moving object comes to rest unless we keep pushing it. Have them tell you why it comes to rest and how you might make it travel farther without pushing it more. Extend this to some everyday occurrences, such as in cycling. Ask about the role of oil in reducing friction and suggest the children feel the effect of a drop of cooking oil on a surface. (The paper towels are to clean their hands and the table-top afterwards.)

Talk: *Watch me give a push to this car. What happens? Why doesn't it keep going? If this was a real car, would that be what we want? So, sometimes, friction is something we don't want. When you are on your bicycle, going along on the level, what do you have to do to keep going? What happens if you don't keep pedalling? There is something you do now and again·to keep the friction down in your bicycle wheels. Can you remember what it is? You put some oil in the wheel axle. How does that help? Let's check your idea. Push your finger on the table and see how much friction there is. I'm going to put a drop of cooking oil on the table. Try it again with the cooking oil. What does it feel like?*

More to talk about and do

Streamlining

The steps above focus on friction between solids. You should extend the ideas to include friction in air and water. This is an 'all around' friction that is reduced by giving things a smooth, slim shape we call *streamlining*. In water, fish generally have this shape. In air, most cars and large aircraft are streamlined. Ask the children what shape we should be if we wanted to run faster.

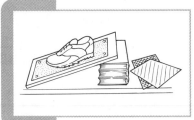

FIGURE 4.18

Hands-on: shoes and friction

Ask the children to compare:
▶ the friction between different surfaces and the sole of a shoe, by fixing the material to a board and tilting it with a shoe on it. The bigger the angle at which the shoe slips, the more friction there is (see Figure 4.18).

▶ the friction between one surface and the soles of different shoes, by placing them on a board and tilting it (which has the most grip?); the one that slides last has the most grip (see Figure 4.19).

You could use Photocopiable Thinksheets 32 and 33 on pages 149 and 150 to structure these activities for the children. For the first, you will need to provide off-cuts of various floor coverings. For the second, you will need to make available three or four shoes with different kinds of sole.

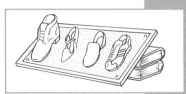

FIGURE 4.19

Hands-on: friction and heat

If you wish to show children that friction produces heat, ask them to touch the tip of their noses with an eraser to sense its temperature, then rub it fairly vigorously on a surface for a few seconds and try it again. They will find that the eraser feels warm after rubbing.

Checking for understanding

Check on the children's understanding with questions and tasks, such as:

▶ *In winter, the footpaths are sometimes slippery. Why? Sand can be spread on them so that people do not slip. Why does that work? What does it do to the friction?*

▶ *Suppose you made a buggy. When you try it out, you find it will not go far. What are some of the things you would try to make it go farther? Why do you think they would help?*

▶ Set up a simple pendulum using a small clay ball on a string. *Why does it not swing forever?* (Note: those in some clocks keep going for a long time because they get a push from the spring or the battery. When the spring unwinds or the battery is flat, the clock pendulum stops.)

Related topics
▶ Forces (page 124).

Gravity

What is gravity?

All objects attract one another, but this attraction is minute when the objects are small. A table, a chair and even a house are far too small for their pull to be noticeable. The Earth, however, is big enough to attract things to its surface. Stones, soil and people are examples of some of what the Earth attracts. We call this pull to the Earth the *force of gravity*. A big stone has more material in it than a small stone. The force of gravity on the big stone is bigger than the force of gravity on the small stone. If you hang the big stone on a spring, the force of gravity pulls the stone down and the spring stretches. If you hang the small stone on the spring, the force of gravity is less and so the spring does not stretch as much. We say the big stone weighs more than the small stone. Weight is a measure of the force of gravity on something. An adult weighs more than a small child because the force of gravity is bigger on the adult.

Mass and weight are often confused. *Mass* is the amount of material in something. *Weight* is the pull of gravity on it. The more mass there is in something, the bigger the pull of gravity on it and we say it weighs more. Mass is the same everywhere, but the pull of gravity (weight) depends on where you are. Suppose your schoolbag amounted to 6kg of mass. On the Earth, gravity would pull on it with roughly 6kg of force. On the Moon, gravity would pull with only 1kg of force. Far out in space, the pull on it could be almost nothing. But, in all these places, the mass of the bag would be 6kg because it has the same amount of material in it.

Understanding gravity

Children have lived with gravity since before they were born. What could be more natural than things falling to the surface of the Earth? They see nothing special about gravity – it is just how things are. Children usually pass through a phase when they ask 'Why?' about everything, but they rarely ask why things fall down. To them, there is nothing to explain. The aim is to help them notice the effects of the pull of gravity and to see that there is something to explain.

Steps to understanding

The approach taken here is to draw children's attention to the peculiar behaviour of objects on the Earth's surface. A simple analogy is introduced to explain it. Analogies only work if the children are familiar with their basis. A step is included to do that, but you may feel it is not needed with some children. Analogies are never perfect and their faults have to be pointed out. That is done in another step.

Age range and duration
The approach is suitable for intermediate and older children in the primary school. Putting aside written and other tasks you may want to include, allow between one and two hours for the steps, depending on how many you use.

Step 1: Falling things
This step calls for some feigned surprise on your part. Show the children some everyday items, such as a piece of chalk, an eraser, a small stone. Ask them to identify them, then hold them out in your hand and let them fall. At the same time, look up, as though expecting them to rise. Is this what most things do? What makes them fall?

Talk: *Oh! Which way did they go? Why did none of them go up? Or sideways? If you step off a chair, which way do you go? Have you ever gone up and kept on going? Why do you always end up going down? Why do most things end down there? Look around us. Tell me some of the things that are down there. Do we have to nail them down? Are stones glued down? So why do they stay down? The planet Earth that we live on is very big* (show a globe and a tiny dot on it to represent a child). *It pulls stones and things like that down on to it. They don't have to be fastened down because they are held there by the invisible pull of the Earth. We call this pull 'gravity'.* (Photocopiable Thinksheet 34 on page 151 helps the children play with the idea of gravity in a way that highlights what we take for granted.)

Step 2: The basis of an analogy
You will need a long elastic band, cut open to make a long, string-like piece. Discuss, through questions, what it is, how it behaves and what it feels like.

Talk: *What's this? What happens when I pull it? Tell me what it feels like? What will happen if I let go?*

FIGURE 4.20

toy figure

elastic band

Step 3: Using the rubber band analogy to 'explain' gravity
You will need a toy figure, large enough for all to see clearly. Attach one end of the length of elastic band used in Step 2 firmly to the figure's feet. Attach the other end firmly to a flat surface, such as a table-top. The Figure represents a child and the flat surface represents the surface of the Earth. When the 'child' stands on a chair (a pile of books), it stretches the elastic band. When the 'child' steps off, the band pulls the Figure down to the surface of the Earth (Figure 4.20). Discuss the effect with the children.

Talk: *Can you see what I've done? I've fastened the elastic band to her feet. Now she's climbing onto the chair. See, she's standing on it. This is a bit like gravity. We can't see gravity but we can see what's happening to the elastic band. It's pulling on her. If I let go, she is pulled to the ground, just like you jumping off a chair. Things fall down as if they had an elastic band that joined them to the Earth.*

Step 4: The limits of the elastic band analogy
The pull of an elastic band is greater the more you stretch it. This is not the case with gravity. It does not become stronger if you jump higher. This has to be conveyed to the children, using the toy figure of Step 3.

Talk: *I said that this is a bit like gravity. It helps us understand gravity, but there isn't really an invisible elastic band tied around our feet, is there? There's something* *else that's different. The higher she jumps* (referring to the toy figure) *the more the elastic band pulls. Feel it for yourself. However, gravity doesn't pull harder the higher you jump. You could jump as high as a house and gravity would not pull down harder. You would hurt yourself more, of course, because you would have more time to build up speed.*

More to talk about and do
Mass, gravity and weight
If you decide to explain the difference between mass and weight, it is pointless if the words mean nothing to the children, even if they are scientific and correct. Keep it simple, concrete and support it with visual aids. Obtain a house brick and a different brick, such as one used for paving. Stand the house brick on some bathroom scales. This tells us its weight and this is the size of the Earth's pull on the house brick. Mass is the amount of material in the brick. If the paving brick has more mass than the house brick (more material in it), the Earth's pull on it will be greater. Weighing it will let us know if it has more mass. We may even be able to tell just by holding the bricks in our hands. That lets us feel the size of the Earth's pull on the bricks.

Hands-on: measuring the force of gravity
Bathroom scales are useful for measuring the force of gravity on things. The more gravity pulls down on something, the more it squashes the scales and gives a bigger reading. *What kinds of things have big gravity forces on them? Is the force of gravity on you more after you have had a meal?* Questions like this are readily answered using bathroom scales.

Checking for understanding
Check on the children's understanding with questions and tasks, such as:
▶ *We always say we fall down. Why don't we fall up?*
▶ *People who decorate houses use a plumb line to make sure that they keep the wallpaper vertical. A plumb line is a long string with a small, heavy object on the end. How is it able to make a vertical line?* (The object on the plumb line was always made of lead because lumps of lead are heavy – hence plumb line from the Latin *plumbus*, meaning lead.)
▶ *If I stand a toy car on the carpet, it makes dents in the carpet where the wheels are. If I stand another car on the top of it, the dents are deeper. Why? What has it to do with gravity?*

> **Related topics**
> ▶ Forces (page 124)
> ▶ Magnetism (page 133).

Light sources

What are sources of light?
Some things produce light themselves. A torch, a match, a candle, an electric lamp, a fire, a luminous watch, and the Sun and other stars all produce light. In a candle flame, for instance, the burning substances become very hot and glow, giving off light. In a luminous watch, the special paint absorbs light energy by day then it gives off light in the dark so we can see the hands or digits. The candle flame and the paint produce light. Other objects do not make light but only reflect the light that falls on them. The Moon, a white sheet of paper, a mirror and cats' eyes are examples. We see the Moon because of the sunlight that falls on it and bounces off towards our eyes. Without sunlight, the Moon would be almost completely black. We see cats' eyes shining at night because light from car headlights bounces off their eyes towards us. When the car headlights are turned off, cats' eyes no longer shine. These are *reflectors* of light.

Understanding sources of light

Many people find it hard to distinguish between producers and reflectors of light. In particular, reflectors of light are often seen as producing light themselves. For example, children may think that if a mirror or a jewel is taken into a dark cupboard, they will be able to see because these bright objects will light up the room. The aim here is to help the children discriminate between producers and reflectors of light, and to grasp the limitations of the latter.

Steps to understanding

The steps provide a practical approach to learning the distinction between a source of light and a reflector of light.

Age range and duration

The topic is appropriate for both younger and older children. Putting aside written and additional activities you may want to include, allow between one and two hours to complete the steps, depending on the age of the children.

Step 1: Things that make their own light

Show the children some common light producers (for example, draw attention to the Sun's light, the classroom's electric lights and a light from a battery-powered torch). Ask the children to tell you other things that make their own light.

> **Talk:** *Do you know what this is? What does it do? I have a dark cupboard where I keep my books. Could I use the torch to help me find a book I want? If I didn't have a torch, what else could I use? Let's make a list of your ideas.*

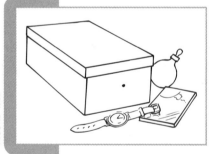

FIGURE 4.21

Step 2: Testing ideas

You will need a shoebox with a small viewing hole at one end (Figure 4.21). This is to be the dark cupboard. You also need a range of safe things to test, for example, a modern luminous watch (old luminous watches may contain radioactive paint and should not be used), a battery-powered torch, a crystal, a tree decoration, and a plastic mirror. These are placed in the box in turn and viewed through the hole.

> **Talk:** *Let's test some things to see what might be useful in a dark cupboard. This box is going to be our cupboard. You can't possibly get inside it, but you can look in through this small hole. That's not a perfect way of doing it because... well, you tell me. That's right, a little bit of light from out here can get in. We'll have to remember that when we look in the box. What about this crystal? Will it make light inside the box? Let's try it.*

Step 3: Things that only reflect light

The children have sorted things into those that make light in the box and those that do not. Using guided discussion you must now give specific attention to those that do not make their own light.

> **Talk:** *Some people think you can see in a dark cupboard with a mirror* (or tinsel, or a crystal, and so on). *Why might people think this? What did we find out? Does a mirror make light itself? No, it's not like a torch. It just lies there. It can't do anything in the dark. There has to be a light maker as well if we are going to see it.*

What's the light maker in our classroom? What things can we see with it? Suppose it went out – could we still see them?

More to talk about and do
Galileo
Galileo, an Italian scientist, was probably the first person to study the night sky with a telescope. For example, he discovered moons in orbit around the planet Jupiter. Jupiter and its moons simply reflect the Sun's light and our eyes can cope with that. But Galileo went on to look at the Sun. This cost him his eyesight. The Sun produces an enormous amount of light and heat which, when they hit the back of the eye, destroy the light-sensitive layer. Warn the children that they should never look directly at the Sun, with or without a telescope.

Hands-on: investigating producers of light
The brightness of light from a torch depends on the state of the battery. A well-used battery is unlikely to produce as much light as a new one. Provide two or three identical torches containing batteries that make the torches have different brightness. Which torch is the brightest? The children have to devise a way of comparing the light from the torches. You could provide them with a large sheet of greaseproof paper. The light from the torches could be shone on one side and the brightness compared from the other side (Figure 4.22).

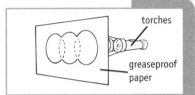
torches
greaseproof paper
FIGURE 4.22

Hands-on: investigating reflectors of light
You will need cards (roughly A4 or A5) in different colours. If, for instance, a yellow card is stood on a white surface and torch light or sunlight falls on it, yellow light will be seen reflected on the white surface (Figure 4.23). The children can see for themselves that different cards produce different effects. More than that, some reflect more light than others. At the extremes, black reflects the least and white the most, so white is a good 'colour' to wear in order to be seen.

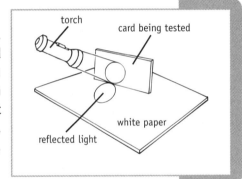
torch
card being tested
white paper
reflected light
FIGURE 4.23

Checking for understanding
Check on the children's understanding with questions and tasks, such as:

▶ *I was sorting out my cupboard and I found this bright shiny thing. I thought it might be a light-maker, but I could be wrong. How could I test it to see if it makes light? Why will that test work?*

▶ *The Sun is a light-maker. The Moon is not. If the Sun went out, what would the Moon look like? Why?*

▶ *Suppose I did not have a light-maker. I want to see inside my dark cupboard. I do have a mirror and the Sun is shining into the room where the dark cupboard is. Is there a way of getting a little light into the cupboard? How could I do it? Why would that work?*

Related topics
▶ Seeing (page 63)
▶ Shadows (page 138)
▶ Mirrors (page 136).

Magnetism

What is the force of magnetism?
A magnet can affect certain materials placed near it. In particular, iron and steel items will be attracted to a magnet and will be pulled to it if they are light enough. This pulling force is invisible and the magnet does not have to touch the object to pull it. (Note that a

magnet will attract a tin can, but that is because it is really a steel can with a thin layer of tin on it to prevent rusting.) Magnets have two parts where the magnetic effect is particularly strong. These are the *poles* of the magnet. Either of these poles will attract an unmagnetised iron or steel object. Nevertheless, the two poles are different and are called the *north* and the *south* poles of the magnet. When two magnets are brought together so that a north and south pole are near one another, the magnets *attract* each other. When two north poles or two south poles are brought near, the magnets *repel* one another and push each other apart. So, magnets are a source of forces. They can pull certain unmagnetised materials and also another magnet if north and south poles are placed near. They can also push another magnet if two north or two south poles are placed near.

Understanding the force of magnetism

Children's experience of forces is largely through those they produce or feel themselves. These generally involve contact so they may think that a magnet has to touch things to attract them. In other words, they may not appreciate that the influence of a magnet spreads out invisibly some distance around it. The aim is to illustrate that magnets are a source of invisible forces and that contact is not needed.

Steps to understanding

The approach taken here is to show that a magnet's influence stretches out into the space around it. A simple explanation is provided using the idea of an invisible hand.

Age range and duration

The approach is suitable for most children, regardless of age, although this topic tends to be taught to intermediate and older primary school children. Putting aside written and additional activities you may want to include among the steps, allow up to an hour, depending on the number of steps you include. (Traditionally, iron filings have been used to show the sphere of influence of a magnet. These are not without danger, particularly if the filings find their way into a child's eye. A safer way of working is described below.)

Step 1: Magnets attract certain materials

You need a tray of safe objects, each with a label indicating the material it is made from (for example, a plastic pen top, steel nail, copper pipe, paper book). The children try the magnet on the materials and classify them into those that are pulled to the magnet and those that are not. This is an exploratory step that the children can often do themselves.

Talk: (Show a magnet.) *Can anyone tell me what this is? Where might we find one?* (For example, kitchen cupboard doors.) *What do they do? What things stick to magnets? Let's find out.*

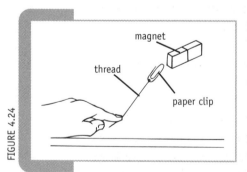

FIGURE 4.24

Step 2: The invisible force of magnetism

You will need a length of thread, a paper clip that will stick to a magnet and a fairly strong magnet. Attach the thread to the clip. Hold the other end of the thread on a table-top. With the magnet in the other hand, let the clip stick to it. Raise it above the table and gently ease the magnet away until it just leaves the clip (Figure 4.24). The clip will be suspended without touching the magnet.

Talk: *Look. I've fastened the clip on a thread. Now it's stuck to the magnet. I'm lifting it up slowly. Now I'm pulling back gently. There! What can you see? Is there* *anything between the magnet and the clip? So the magnet's pulling force is invisible. It's like an invisible hand stretching out from the magnet and pulling on the clip. There isn't really an invisible hand there, is there? It just behaves like that.*

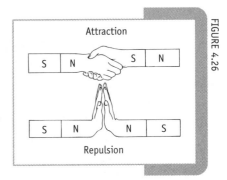

Step 3: Consolidation

You will need the same items as in Step 2 and also a sheet of paper and other thin objects, such as a plastic ruler. With the paper clip suspended in the air, as above, ask a child to slide a sheet of paper between the magnet and the clip. The clip will remain suspended, showing that the invisible force can pass through paper. The other objects can be tested similarly (Figure 4.25).

Talk: *Very carefully slide the paper into the gap. Look. The clip's still being pulled up. What does that tell us?*

Step 4: Working with two magnets to produce both pulls and pushes

You will need two magnets. Begin with them placed so that they attract one another, then place them so that they repel one another.

Talk: *Watch. See how the magnets pull each other together? It's as though they have invisible hands that stretch out and pull each other together. Now watch this. I'm turning one of the magnets around. When I hold this one near it, what happens? This time the magnets are pushing each other apart. It's as though they have invisible hands that meet and push each other apart (Figure 4.26). Of course, there are no invisible hands, are there? It's just a way of helping us think about what happens.*

More to talk about and do

The Earth as a magnet

The Earth behaves as though it has a giant bar magnet inside it. The magnet in a compass is affected by the Earth's 'magnet' and lines itself up roughly north–south. Knowing which way is north and which way is south is useful for finding your way. Pictures that show the Earth with a bar magnet inside it, usually show the magnet tilted to one side. This is because the Earth's magnetism is not lined up exactly north–south and it is why compasses point only roughly north. (Of course, the Earth does not really have a bar magnet inside it. Electrical currents in the Earth's metallic core produce the Earth's magnetism.) Ask the children to find out about the compass and what it does.

Most of the steps above could be done by the children themselves. If you decide this is appropriate, you will need to emphasise that dropping magnets or hitting them together weakens them. In addition, here is another activity they might try.

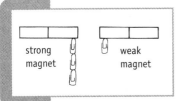

Hands-on: finding the poles of a magnet and comparing magnets

The strongest parts of a magnet may be found by dipping it into a bowl of paper clips and noting where most tend to stick. This usually indicates that the poles of a bar magnet are near its ends. The strength of two magnets can be compared by seeing how many paper clips can be suspended from their poles (see Figure 4.27).

Related topics
- Forces (page 124)
- Materials (page 89)
- Gravity (page 129)
- Seeing (page 63).

Checking for understanding

Check on the children's understanding with questions and tasks, such as:

- *Does a magnet have to touch something to pull on it? How do you know that?*

- *A magnet can pull on things and it can push on things. Can it twist things? Think of how you might make a magnet twist things. Draw a picture to show how you would do it.*

- *Imagine you own a scrap metal business. How could you use a magnet to help you sort the scrap metal? Why would that work?*

Mirrors

What is the reflection of light?

When light hits the page of a book, some bounces off. A scientist would say that some light has been reflected by the page. Light bounces off rough surfaces irregularly. This is rather like the way a ball bounces off an uneven wall. You cannot be sure where the ball will go. Light bounces off smooth, polished surfaces something like a ball bouncing off a smooth wall. You have a good idea which way the ball will go after it hits the wall. The direction of the ball is predictable, so you can be there to catch it. Light behaves in a similar way. This regular behaviour is a pattern of nature. Light behaved like this yesterday, it will do the same today and it will do the same tomorrow (unless the laws of nature change, but we have no reason to expect that to happen).

Understanding the reflection of light from mirrors

Children often do not see the reflection of light in its broader context, that is, reflection from surfaces in general with the mirror as a special case. While most children will agree that mirrors reflect light, they may deny that other surfaces also reflect light. The aim is to link mirror reflection to this broader context.

Steps to understanding

The sequence begins with light bouncing off more or less rough surfaces and ends with light bouncing off very smooth surfaces. The bouncing ball analogy mentioned above is used.

Age range and duration

The topic is appropriate for all children, although you would probably omit the final step with younger children. Putting aside time for written and additional activities you may want to include among the steps, allow up to two hours for them, depending on the age of the children.

Step 1: Introducing the basis of the bouncing ball analogy

You need a ball and access to smooth and rough surfaces for bouncing the ball. The aim is to remind the children that the way the ball bounces is fairly predictable on some surfaces but not on others. You do this by direct demonstration.

Talk: *What's the difference between that wall and that one? Which is the rougher wall? What will happen if I throw the ball at the rougher wall? Do you know which way it will bounce? Let's try it. See if you can catch the ball. Now let's try the smooth wall. Will catching the ball be harder or easier this time? Where will you stand? How do you know where to stand?*

Step 2: Bouncing light from different surfaces

The intention is to compare the quality of the reflection from different surfaces. You will need several sheets of white paper with different kinds of surface (for example, a drawing paper, a glossy paper, a sheet of photocopying paper, a sheet of the latter that you have crumpled and then smoothed by hand) and a battery-powered torch. Arrange things so that the torchlight can be shone on each sample of paper in turn and reflect its light onto another kind of surface (for example, white paper – see Figure 4.28).

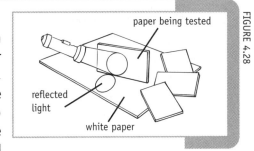

FIGURE 4.28

Talk: *Are these pieces of paper all the same? How are they different? What do they remind you of?* (The different wall surfaces.) *I'm not going to bounce a ball off them; instead, I'm going to see if I can bounce light from the torch off them. Will it bounce? What do you think will happen? See how this one seems to scatter the light everywhere? Why does it do that? See how this smooth, shiny one bounces the light over there? What does that remind you of?* (The bouncing ball activity.) *If you could catch the light bouncing off paper, which kind of paper would be best for the game? Why? Can we put the sheets of paper in order from those that would be best for the game to those that would be worst?*

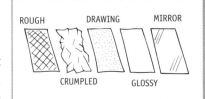

FIGURE 4.29

Step 3: Bouncing light from a mirror

In this step, you extend the children's thinking to include plastic mirror surfaces. Keep the ordered sheets of paper in place as used in Step 2. Show the children a plastic mirror and ask them to examine its appearance. Ask the children to decide where it would fit in the sequence (usually, it goes next to the glossy paper). Test it, as was done with the papers, and show that it is a good reflector, hopefully as the children predicted it would be (Figure 4.29).

Talk: *Look at this. What is it? What does it feel like? Is it rough or smooth? How would the light bounce off this? Why do you think that? If we put it with our pieces of paper, where should it go? Why do you think that? Let's see if you are right. We'll test it with the torch. Is it as good as the glossy paper? Is it better?*

Step 4: Applying what they now know about the reflection of light

In this step, the children use what they know about bouncing light off smooth surfaces to predict where the light will go. You need the torch and the plastic mirror from the previous step. Put the mirror somewhere where the children can see it clearly. Stand a little away from the mirror and prepare to switch the torch on. Ask the children where the light will bounce, then test their predictions.

FIGURE 4.30

Talk: *If I put the mirror there and I shine the torch on it from here, where do you think the light will go? Why do you think it will go there?* (If necessary, ask the children to think in terms of a ball bouncing from a wall.) *Let's see if you are right.* (Repeat this for other angles and positions – Figure 4.30.)

More to talk about and do

Early mirrors

In Ancient Egypt, poor people had to use a bowl of water as a mirror. Rich people had polished metal mirrors. The children could compare the effects of using a dish of water and a plastic mirror.

A law of reflection

These steps could also be used to lead to a law of reflection. This states more formally the idea that was being developed above, namely, the angle the light makes as it approaches a flat mirror is the same as it makes as it leaves the mirror (Figure 4.31). The following activity describes a way of doing this with children.

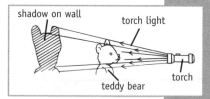

Hands-on: investigating angles in reflection

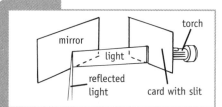

Children do not have to be able to use a protractor to show that the angles involved in reflection from a flat mirror are equal. Provide them with a safe, plastic mirror and a torch. The torch should have a piece of card with a slit in it over the end so that a line of light comes out. The children shine this line of light at a mirror so that it reflects from it (Figure 4.32). They draw along the lines of light and the mirror surface and cut out the angles. These are then laid on top of one another to show they are the same. This is repeated for other angles.

Checking for understanding

Check on the children's understanding with questions and tasks, such as:

▶ *If I sandpapered a mirror so that the surface was rough, would that make a difference to how the light bounced off it. How? Why?*

▶ *Chandrakanta sits in the sun to read her book, but it is too hot. When she tries to read her book behind a wall, it is too dark. She needs more light behind the wall. There is a mirror you can use to help her. Draw a picture to show how you would use the mirror so she could read her book* (see Photocopiable Thinksheet 35 on page 152).

▶ *How could reflections be dangerous to a driver?* (See Photocopiable Thinksheet 35 on page 152.)

Related topics
▶ Seeing (page 63)
▶ Shadows (page 138)
▶ Light sources (page 131).

Shadows

Why are there shadows?

Light flares out from a small torch and heads in straight lines towards a teddy bear (Figure 4.33). The teddy bear blocks some of the light before it reaches the wall. Since that part of the light never gets to the wall, there is a dark patch which we call a *shadow*. The wall is bright elsewhere because light from the torch gets there. The shadow of the teddy bear is bigger than the bear itself because the light flares out in straight lines from the torch, spreading out as it goes past the bear on its way to the wall.

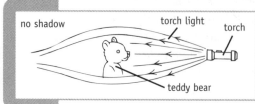

Suppose light did not travel in straight lines but bent around the teddy bear on the way to the wall. If this happened, shadows may not exist at all (Figure 4.34). Since there are shadows like the one in Figure 4.33, light travels in straight lines.

A room often has more than one source of light. The teddy bear may block the light from one source but not from another. Walls may reflect some light into the shadow, too. The result is that shadows are often neither black nor sharp.

Understanding shadows

The children's experience of shadows in the home or classroom can give them the idea that light is able to bend around obstacles, so that shadows are often grey and washed out. In addition, although they see the blurred edges of such shadows, they may not relate them to multiple sources of light. The aim is to help the child grasp the cause of shadows and, if you wish, go on to understand why many shadows are not perfect.

Steps to understanding

The first steps focus on the form and cause of a simple shadow, helping the child to understand it using a water-spray analogy. You may then go on to consider the causes of multiple shadows.

Age range and duration

Use the steps that are appropriate for the children you teach. For instance, the first two steps and the last step (about the limitations of the analogy) could make an introductory unit. The other steps then extend the idea for older children. Putting aside time for written and additional activities among the steps, allow half an hour for the truncated version and a further half an hour for the remaining steps.

Step 1: Observing a simple shadow

Ask the children to observe a simple shadow, such as that produced by a small, bright torch (as in Figure 4.33). Ask them to speculate about its cause. They will probably be able to argue that the obstacle blocks the light. Take it further to help them grasp why the shadow is the same shape as the obstacle but bigger. This allows you to find out their ideas about how light moves from the torch to the wall. Do they think in terms of straight lines (and hence explain the size of the shadow) or do they think in terms of curves?

> **Talk:** *What's that? Why is it dark? Why can't the light get there? What is its shape like? Why is it bigger?*

Step 2: Introducing a water-spray analogy for light

You will need a hand-operated water spray to demonstrate this analogy. The best kind have an adjustable nozzle that allows you to produce a divergent spray of water that can lightly wet a vertical surface. Some household hand sprays may be suitable if they have been rinsed thoroughly. Spray at a waterproof obstacle so that a damp area surrounding a dry patch is produced on a wall or window (as in Figure 4.35). The analogy can help you show that the shadow is bigger than the obstacle because light 'flares out' and goes 'straight to the wall', just like the water.

FIGURE 4.35

> **Talk:** *How is this like the torch and shadow? What is like the torch? What is like the shadow? What is like the light? Why is the part like the shadow the same shape as the teddy? Why is it bigger? So, the water comes out of the spout and flares out as it goes straight across to the wall. Look, I'll put the torch on again. What do you think the light must be doing? It must flare out like the water did. So why is the shadow bigger? It keeps on flaring out, straight past the shape and up to the wall.*

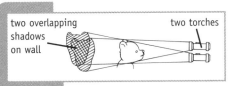

two overlapping shadows on wall   two torches

FIGURE 4.36

Step 3: Making a double shadow

Now make a more complex shadow using two torches (Figure 4.36). Ask the children to try to explain what they see. Encourage them to think in terms of the analogy.

Talk: *What's happening here? How is it different? Why is it like that?*

FIGURE 4.37

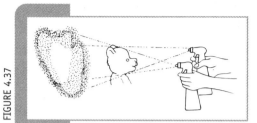

Step 4: Explaining a double shadow using the analogy

Return to the analogy. Produce one 'shadow' with a spray in one hand, then produce another, overlapping 'shadow' with a spray in the other hand (Figure 4.37). What should have been a dry patch from the first spray now has some water on it. You should draw parallels with what you did in Step 3: the water makes two, overlapping patches – the light from the two torches also made two overlapping patches.

Talk: *Watch. There's our 'shadow'. See, it's dry in the middle. That's like one torch. Now, we want another torch. Here's another spray. There, that's another water shadow. Look closely at them. What do you see? So the second one spoiled the first one. How do you think it did that? Let's have a look at the torches again. There's the first one switched on and there's its shadow. Now, what do you think will happen when I switch on the second one? Let's see. How is that like the water sprays? The light from the second one gets into the shadow of the first. It's like two shadows overlapping.*

Step 5: Some limits of the water spray analogy

You should discuss some limits of the water spray analogy, so that the children do not think that light beams are made up of droplets of light that eventually curve down to the ground, like water from a hose pipe.

Talk: *Torch light behaves a bit like a water spray, but not exactly like it. Can you think of any differences?*

More to talk about and do

Shadows in sunlight and on a dull day

The sun tends to give sharp shadows because it is so far away that it behaves like a very, very bright, small torch. On a fairly dull day, the whole of the sky behaves like a wide source of light so light can get everywhere and shadows are faint or non-existent.

Hands-on: why does the shadow get smaller as you move the teddy away from the wall?

Show how shadow size varies, according to the distance of the object from the wall. Move it close to the wall and the shadow will be small; move it away and it grows. *Why is that? How does the size (diameter) of the shadow depend on the distance from the wall? Where would the obstacle have to be for the shadow to be the same size as the obstacle?* Ask the children to measure the shadow and the distance from the wall. They could draw a graph of their results and explain what it shows. Ask them to use the water spray analogy to help them explain.

Checking for understanding

Check on the children's understanding with questions and tasks, such as:

▶ *Faysal stands near the lamp. Why is the shadow bigger than Faysal?* (See Photocopiable Thinksheet 36 on page 153.)
▶ *Tell me why the shadows made by the classroom lights are so fuzzy. Why do the shadows that the sun makes have sharper edges*

Related topics
▶ Seeing (page 63)
▶ Mirrors (page 136)
▶ Light sources (page 131).

than the shadows made by the classroom lights?

▶ *How can you make two shadows of a vase at the same time? Can you make them overlap? Why does that work? (See Photocopiable Thinksheet 36 on page 153.)*

Sound

What is the cause of sound?

Sound is produced by things that vibrate. If you pluck a guitar string, it vibrates and we hear a sound. If you drop a metal dustbin lid, it vibrates and we hear the clatter. Rapid vibrations make high-pitched sounds; slow vibrations make low-pitched sounds. A thin, taut guitar string tends to vibrate quickly and so it produces a high note. A string that is thick and heavy vibrates more slowly and makes a low note. A dustbin lid often vibrates in lots of different ways at once and usually makes an unpleasant mix of sounds that we call a *noise*. The loudness of the sound depends on, among other things, the size of the vibration. Bigger vibrations generally make louder sounds because they send out stronger pulses in the air.

Understanding the cause of sound

The children's problem with sound is that it is invisible. At the same time, sources of sound can vibrate so quickly that children do not see the vibrations or relate them to the pitch and the loudness of the sound. As a consequence, they may not relate sound and vibrating objects. They need to be convinced that things making sounds are vibrating, in spite of appearances, and that the rate and size of the vibrations matter.

Steps to understanding

▶ Steps 1 and 2 aim to convince children that vibrations and sound go together.
▶ Steps 3 and 4 relate the size of the vibration to the loudness of the sound and the rate of the vibration to the pitch of the sound.
▶ Step 5 consolidates learning.

Age range and duration

Altogether, these steps could be incorporated in lessons lasting a total of three hours. You are unlikely to teach them in a continuous block so try them in three, roughly equal parts: the first two steps, the second two steps and then the last step. All but the very youngest children could probably cope with first three steps. The remaining steps are better suited to older children.

FIGURE 4.38

Step 1: showing that a tuning fork vibrates when it makes a sound

You will need a tuning fork and a beaker of water. Make the tuning fork emit a sound by hitting the tines (prongs) on a book. The sound will be more audible if you press the heel of the fork to a table-top. As the children attend to the sound, they should watch the fork's tines closely. The prongs will look a little blurred as they vibrate. Show the children that the prongs are vibrating by dipping the tines into water immediately after they have been struck (Figure 4.38).

Talk: *Watch!* (Strike the fork on a book and touch the heel to a table-top.) *Listen! What's it doing? I'll do it again. Look closely at the prongs. What's happening? What are the prongs doing? It looks as though they might be shaking, doesn't it? How can we be sure they are shaking? I'll hit it again. Touch the prongs very, very gently with a finger. Did you feel anything? Watch. I'll hit it again and dip it into some water.*

Why did it do that? What does that tell us? Does it make a sound when the prongs aren't shaking? Let's try it. No, you are right, it doesn't. So, what have we found out? Shaking and sound go together. Another word for shaking like this is called 'vibrating'. Vibrating and sound go together. When things vibrate we often get sounds. Can you think of a new sentence with 'vibrate' and 'sound' in it?

Step 2: Showing that other things vibrate when they make a sound

You need, for example, a drum, cymbals, a triangle and a battery-powered radio. In all cases, the vibrations they produce may be felt by gentle touch. Dipping the sounding cymbals and triangle in water can also show they are vibrating, just like the tuning fork. If the drum is large and resonates for some time after it has been struck, the vibrations will make a small, crumpled piece of paper on its surface jump.

Talk: *When I hit the drum, it makes a sound. Does it shake? Does it vibrate? How do we know? How could we test it to see if it shakes and vibrates? What about the cymbals? How could we test those? What about the triangle? How could we test it? Here's a radio. We can't dip it in water because it uses electricity. How could we test it to see if it vibrates when it makes a noise?*

Step 3: Relating the size of the vibration to the loudness of the sound.

You will need a ruler. A metal ruler is generally best. Hold one end of the ruler firmly on the edge of a table so that about two-thirds of the ruler's length projects. Press the end of the ruler to make a vibration and hence a sound. Now press the end strongly and ask the children to note the difference in loudness. (You could use Photocopiable Thinksheet 37 on page 154 to extend the work on loudness.)

Talk: *What's the ruler doing? How is it like our tuning fork? Does it make a sound when it stands still? What is the difference when it makes a loud sound and a quiet sound? If I want a loud sound, what should I do?*

Step 4: Relating the rate of vibration and the pitch of the sound

You will need something to make a high-pitched note, such as a whistle, and something to make a low note, such as a gong. You also need the ruler used in Step 3. After using the whistle and gong to illustrate a high and low note, place a long length of the ruler over the edge of the table and make it vibrate. Ask the children to listen to the pitch of the note. Repeat the procedure with progressively shorter lengths of the ruler projecting over the edge of the table.

Talk: *The whistle makes what we call a high note; listen. The gong makes what we call a low note; listen. Being high or low has nothing to do with its height – it tells us what kind of note it is.* (Continue with the long length of rule over the edge of the table.) *Is that a high note or a low note?* (Now reduce its length.) *Is this note higher or lower than the last one? What about this one? Higher still. And this? Higher still. Look at the ruler as it makes a high note. Now look at it making a low note. What's different? It's longer and... look at how fast it is shaking. Slow shaking makes low notes and what makes high notes? So slow vibrations make low notes and fast vibrations make high notes.*

Step 5: Apply the new understanding to the piano (or similar instrument).

This is a consolidating step for which you could use a piano with the back removed to reveal the strings, or a guitar or similar stringed instrument. First, make the children aware of the strings and the differences in them (length, tautness and thickness). Next, show how the instrument makes a note. Finally, ask the children to predict the kind of note the various strings will make. Test their predictions directly.

Talk: *Look, the wires – we call them strings – are different. How are they different? Some are longer than the others and some are thicker than the others. If we want them to make a sound, what will they have to do? Shake, vibrate. Look at how the piano does it. When I press a key, a little hammer comes up and hits the string. Can you see it vibrate? Why are some strings thicker than others? What kind of note will they make? Why do you think that? Why are some longer than others? What kind of note will they make? Why do you think that? Why are some tighter than others? What difference will being stretched tight make to how fast it vibrates? What will that do to the note? If I make the hammer hit a string hard, what difference will that make? Why do you think that?*

More to talk about and do

Vibrations from people
People can make a noise, but do they vibrate? The answer is, yes, they do. Our voice boxes (the lumps in our throats) contain stretched bits of material (vocal chords) that vibrate to make a sound. You may sometimes feel the vibrations when someone with a prominent voice box says, 'Aaaaaah'.

Hands-on: does size matter?
Usually, small bells will vibrate more quickly than their big relatives, so the small bells make the higher notes. Often small things produce higher notes than larger versions of the same thing. This is something children can find out for themselves. You need a range of items that come in different sizes, such as: the bars of a xylophone, the tubes of wind chimes, bells and plastic plant pots. Ask the children to tap the large and small versions of each. What did they notice about the notes?

FIGURE 4.39

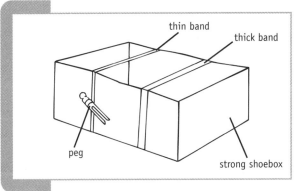

thin band

thick band

peg

strong shoebox

Hands-on: thick and thin, taut and slack – does it matter?
The children can investigate the effect of string thickness and tension using a variety of elastic bands stretched over an empty shoebox. When plucked, the bands emit a note, the thicker ones generally giving the lower notes. When the bands are stretched more, the pitch of the note rises because the band vibrates faster (Figure 4.39).

Checking for understanding
Check on the children's understanding with questions and tasks, such as:
▶ *If I hit a bar on the xylophone, it makes a sound. Why does it do that? What must be happening? Can you think of a way we might test that idea?*
▶ *The bars on the xylophone give different notes. Why do they do that?*
▶ *The door of my car used to make an awful noise as I drove along. When I pressed my hand on it, the noise stopped. Why was that?*

Related topics
▶ Hearing (page 53).

Echoes

Making echoes

This picture shows Mary as she shouts at a wall and listens to the echo.

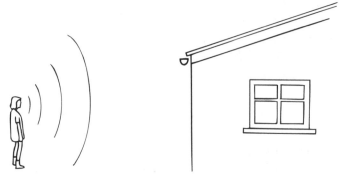

The second picture shows Mary farther from the wall.

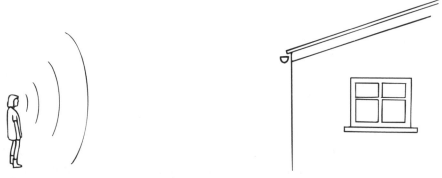

When Mary shouts this time, how will the echo be different?

1 Will it be quieter or louder or just the same as before? Why do you think that?

2 Will the echo come back sooner or later or just the same as before? Why do you think that?

Using echoes

Sometimes, fishermen use sound to find fish. They have a machine that sends out beeps into the water. The fishermen listen for the echoes.

How does this tell them how far they are from the fish?

Spot the faults

The picture below shows an electrical circuit that someone made for a bicycle lamp. It does not work.

1 How many things can you find wrong with the electrical circuit? Draw a ring around each place where there is a fault.

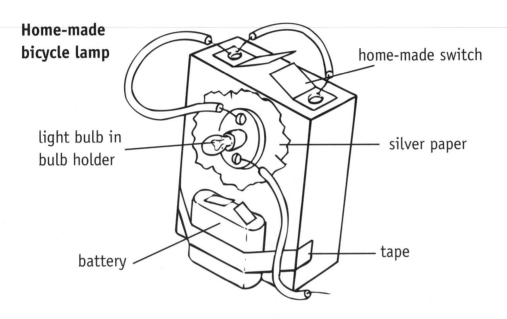

Home-made bicycle lamp

light bulb in bulb holder

home-made switch

silver paper

battery

tape

2 Show me how to make a bicycle lamp that will work. Draw it below. Make sure you connect the wires so that there are no faults.

Electrical circuits

Energy

How does the buggy work?

The picture shows a homemade buggy. It has a long, springy stick with a string on the end. Can you see how the string goes through a hole and is wrapped around the axle of the back wheels?

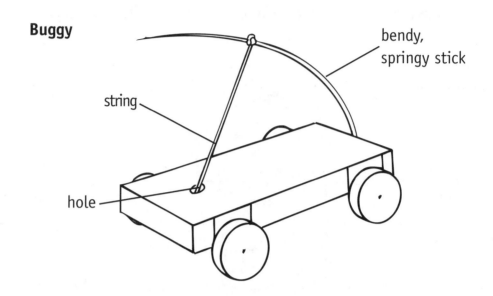

Buggy

bendy, springy stick

string

hole

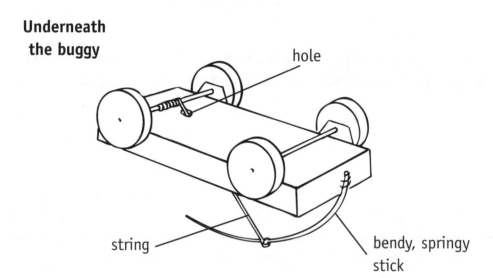

Underneath the buggy

hole

string

bendy, springy stick

1 Is there something ready to change? What is it?

2 When it does change, what will it do?

3 How does the buggy work?

4 Why do the wheels turn round?

5 How would you know if there was any energy left (anything ready to change left)?

Finding the floaters

This picture shows some things that have been put in a dish of water.

**1 Which are floating?
Write a letter F next to
each one that is
floating.
2 Which are not
floating? Write a letter S
next to each one that is
not floating.**

How King Dugall the Sailor became King Dugall the Sinker

King Dugall lived on a small island. His people kept sheep. They sailed to other islands in small boats and traded sheep's wool for fancy goods. King Dugall was miserable. The other kings had big ships and he wanted one too.

One day, he decided to build a ship. It would be bigger than anyone else's ship. But there were no trees on his island. All he had were sheepskins and some bendy branches. So, he used these and built a ship like the one in the picture. It was the biggest ship around.

Everyone on the island was excited. They all dashed down to the beach and climbed into the boat. The boat made a big dent in the water. In fact, the dent was so big that the water came up to the edge of the boat. King Dugall did not want to be left out – after all, it was his boat! So, he waded out and climbed in. The boat made one great 'Bloop!' and sank. Everyone swam to the shore and looked back at where their great ship had been. Now, there was only empty sea.

After that, the other kings called King Dugall the Sailor, King Dugall the Sinker.

**1 Why did the ship not sink when the islanders climbed in?
2 How would you change the boat so that it would not sink when the king climbed in?**

Forces

Sorting forces

• •

These pictures have a push or a pull in them.

1 Which ones show a push?
2 Which ones show a pull?
Write PUSH or PULL under each picture.

3 Think of something else with a pull in it.
4 Think of something else with a push in it.
5 Draw both of these in the empty spaces above.

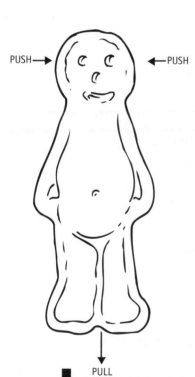

PUSH→ ←PUSH

PULL

This is a picture of a jelly baby sweet. The arrows show where there are going to be push and pull forces on the jelly baby.

6 What shape will it be when it is pushed and pulled like this? Draw it next to the picture

Shoes and floors 1

Friction

Which floor covering would give your shoes the most grip?
Your teacher will give you some different kinds of floor covering.

1 Try feeling them. Which one do you think will have the most grip?

2 Why do you think that?

3 How would you test the floor coverings to see if you are right?
Think of an experiment that will test the floor coverings so that you
will know which one has the most grip. Draw a picture to show how
you will test a floor covering.

4 Write some sentences that describe what you will do in your
experiment.

_____

_____

_____

_____

5 Ask your teacher if you can do your experiment. If you can, make a
list of your results here.

Floor covering	Result

6 What do these results tell you?

Friction

Shoes and floors 2

Which shoe has the most grip?
Your teacher will arrange for you to see some shoes.

1 Look at the soles of the shoes. Which looks as though it would have the most grip?

2 Why do you think that?

3 How would you test the shoes to see if you are right? Think of an experiment that will test the shoes so that you will know which one has the most grip. Draw a picture to show how you will test a shoe.

4 Write some sentences that describe what you will do in your experiment.

_____

_____

_____

_____

5 Ask your teacher if you can do your experiment. If you can, make a list of your results here.

Shoe	Result

6 What do these results tell you?

Lauren and Nadya go into space

Lauren and Nadya won a trip in the Space Shuttle. Something went wrong and they landed on a strange world. Lauren said they should have something to eat before exploring. Things did not happen on that world like they do on the Earth. Lauren opened a tin of peaches, and the peaches fell upwards and hit the ceiling with a splat. Nadya was so surprised that she dropped her spoon. It fell up and bounced on the ceiling. Each bounce became smaller and smaller until the spoon lay there, next to the peaches on the ceiling.

"I know what this is," said Lauren. "We've landed on an anti-gravity world!"

Lauren and Nadya put on their space suits and set off to explore this strange world. Write the next part of the story yourself. Remember, this is an anti-gravity world. Write about something that happened that involved anti-gravity.

_____

_____

_____

_____

_____

_____

_____

_____

_____

_____

Mirrors

Chandrakanta needs more light

Chandrakanta sits in the sun to read her book, but it is too hot. She sees how shady and cool it is behind the wall so she sits there. But, when she tries to read her book behind the wall, it is too dark.

Chandrakanta wants to stay in the shade where it is cool. But there is not enough light for her to read. Would a mirror help? Could a mirror bounce some of the bright light on to her book?

The picture above shows Chandrakanta sitting in the shade. On the picture, draw a mirror that would bounce some of the light from the sun onto her book. Draw a line from the sun to the mirror and then from the mirror to the book to show which way the light would go.

Dangerous lights

The picture below shows a car on a dark night. The car is going down a street where there are shops with big windows. The driver has his headlights on. Some of the light goes up the street and towards the shop window. It will bounce off the glass, but which way?

1 On the picture, draw which way it will bounce.
2 Why might the bouncing light be dangerous?

Faysal's shadow

In the picture, Faysal is sitting at a table, reading and writing. There is a tall lamp nearby. Faysal thinks it will help him read better.

1 Where will his shadow be? Draw it on the picture.
2 Why is the shadow bigger than Faysal? Write your answer under the picture.
3 Where should Faysal put the lamp so that he could see well? Draw it on the picture.
4 Where would Faysal's new shadow be?

Making more shadows

The picture shows a torch, a vase and the shadow of the vase on the wall.

1 How could you make another shadow of the vase near the first shadow? Draw what you would do on the picture.
2 How could you make the second shadow move so that it was partly on top of the first shadow? Write your answer under the picture.

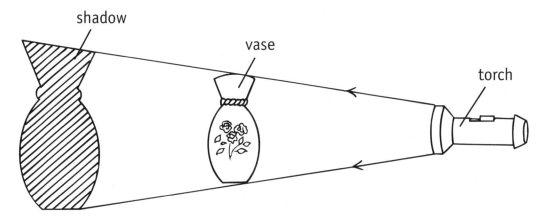

Sound

How loud is it?

Scientists measure how loud a sound is with a decibel meter, like the one in the picture. Below the picture are some measurements it can make.

0 decibels	silence
10 decibels	a leaf scratching along the road
20 decibels	whispering so those nearby can hear
30 decibels	one person talking quietly
40 decibels	a few people talking quietly in the classroom
50 decibels	people talking normally in the classroom
60 decibels	normal road traffic
70 decibels	a train
80 decibels	lorry traffic in the street
90 decibels	thunder
100 decibels	an aeroplane taking off
130 decibels	so loud it hurts
160 decibels	a space rocket taking off

1 Why would people want to measure the loudness of sound?

2 Think of something else that makes a noise of about 10 decibels. What is it you have thought of?

3 Think of something else that makes a noise of about 50 decibels. What is it you have thought of?

4 Think of something else that makes a noise of about 90 decibels. What is it you have thought of?

5 People sometimes talk about noise pollution. What do you think this means?

6 When noise is so loud that it may injure our ears and make us deaf, we have to wear ear defenders. What are ear defenders?

7 Suppose you had to make your ear defenders for yourself. How would do it? Draw a picture and write about what you would use.

Chapter 5
Constructing your own steps to understanding

Why construct steps to understanding yourself?

Constructing steps to help children understand science better is rewarding. You exercise your creativity, put something of yourself into the lesson and feel the satisfaction of seeing it work. Figure 5.1 summarises what to do.

FIGURE 5.1

Constructing steps into science

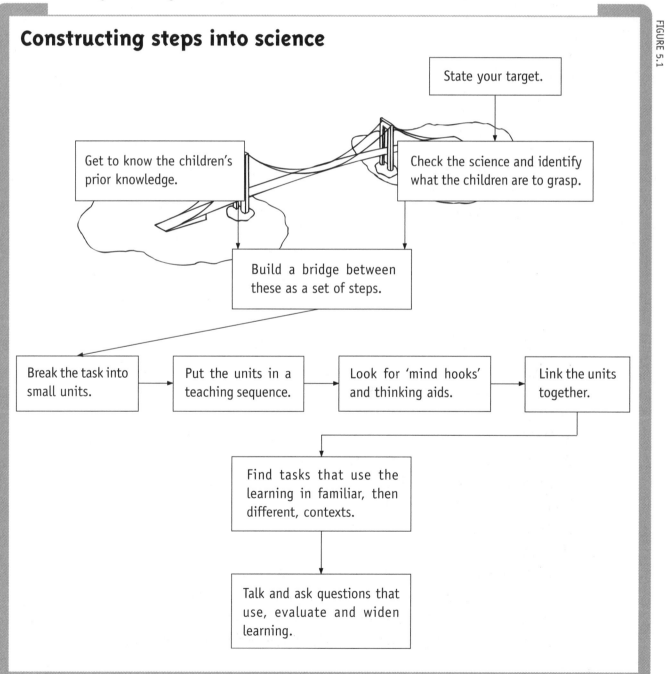

State your target.

Get to know the children's prior knowledge.

Check the science and identify what the children are to grasp.

Build a bridge between these as a set of steps.

Break the task into small units.

Put the units in a teaching sequence.

Look for 'mind hooks' and thinking aids.

Link the units together.

Find tasks that use the learning in familiar, then different, contexts.

Talk and ask questions that use, evaluate and widen learning.

How to go about it

Clarify your goal or target

You need to be clear about your goal or target. If you are vague about what you want to achieve, lessons can lose direction and purpose. A lack of clarity can result in confused and shallow learning. Given the effort you put into a lesson and the time it takes, you want more. The target will probably be set for you either by the teaching programme or your scheme of work. Ask yourself, what exactly does this target mean?

Check the science

Next, quickly check your books to pin down the science. For instance, your programme may say you should teach about simple electrical circuits that include light bulbs, batteries and switches. The question is: teach what? You could include:

▶ how to make a circuit to light a bulb
▶ the concepts of a complete circuit, open circuit and short circuit
▶ the effect of adding more batteries
▶ the effect of adding more bulbs (in series and in parallel)
▶ switches
▶ how a torch works
▶ fitting lights to a model house
▶ making a flashing light for a model pedestrian crossing
▶ Morse code and communication
▶ the invention of the battery
▶ the invention of the light bulb
▶ safety and the mains supply.

And so it goes on. A meaningful grasp of the concept of a complete circuit is central to understanding. This must be a prime target. Having introduced the subject of electricity, it would be wise to make safety and the mains supply an early target, too.

Find out the children's ideas about the topic

Experience will have taught you what the children are capable of and what they already know about topics like electricity. Research on children's ways of thinking about the world is also quite extensive and detailed. Both experience and research were used to help construct the steps in this book. You, however, have an advantage: you can ask the children in front of you what their ideas are. This means that the steps you construct will be tailored precisely to the needs of those you teach.

Construct a path to your target

Your aim is to connect what the children know to where you want them to go. Usually, you will begin with what the children already know and explore the way they see things. At times, you will be able to do something that surprises them, contradicts what they thought would happen and sets up a problem to solve.

Next, take your target, break it down and think about how you will explain its underlying ideas. You may recall what was said in the Introduction – try:

▶ making the invisible visible
▶ making the abstract concrete
▶ using an analogy.

Always fill in the gaps and talk about the science.

For example, the uptake of water by a plant is generally invisible. You could place a stick of celery in coloured water and, after a while, cut across the stem to reveal the path the water has taken. Similarly, you could make abstract language concrete by thinking of everyday instances that are familiar to the children. For instance, in the topic of evaporation, you could talk about what happens to the water in wet hair as it dries. On the other hand, when explaining how light reflects from a mirror, you may remind the children of the way a fast ball bounces off a wall. Analogies are particularly useful as they give people a tool to think with. There are three kinds of analogy:

▶ analogies of appearance ('the Earth is like an orange' – they have the same shape);
▶ analogies of function ('the heart behaves like a pump' – they do the same kind of task but do not look alike);
▶ analogies of appearance and function '('the electrical circuit is like a water circuit using a soap dispenser' – there are similarities in appearance and function).

The last is usually the most powerful kind of analogy but, unfortunately, it can also be hard to find. However, no analogy is effective if the children are not familiar with it. If necessary, spend some time developing the children's grasp of the analogy before you use it. Also, remember that few analogies are perfect. The final step is to point out their limitations.

Think about what you will say
Having put the steps in order and fitted them with mind-grabbing hooks, decide what you will say in each step. Often, people decide what they will *do* but not what they will *say*. What you say is important – success often depends on it. This does not mean that you will be inflexible, relentlessly following a script that has plainly been superseded by the children's responses. It does mean, though, that you will not be fumbling around for the right words and lose the impact of your lesson. Think of words that are meaningful to the children and link them more and more to the new words you want them to use. For example, you may begin by describing how a cymbal is *shaking*. Then you use it in conjunction with *vibrating*. Later, you fade out the use of *shaking*.

Activities
At this stage, you have steps but it is not yet a well-worn path for the children. You will have, however, a variety of activities described in your books and also those that you commonly use. Many will consolidate and extend the children's learning and add to their hands-on experience. Select the best and ask the children to do them. What you have to say, however, is still important so plan your interaction with the children.

Check for understanding
You need to know how well the children understand the topic. Invent some questions that exercise their understanding. While facts are important (we could not think without them), you also need 'why' questions. They make the children think rather than just recycle your words. A bonus is that this questioning also develops learning. For example, you could:

▶ ask the children to express things in their own words and in pictures
▶ ask a child to explain another child's response
▶ ask for another example
▶ ask the children to use what they know to make a prediction and then justify it.

Safety
While being creative, do not forget to think about and plan for safety for yourself, the children and others.

Take opportunities to make connections
Finally, take opportunities to remind children of the science and to use it in new contexts.

Index

● ●

vocal chords 143
hygiene 39, 47, 58, 59, 60
hypotheses *see* prediction; testing

Ice 92–3, 93, 94, 102, 110
ideas (children's) 4, 6, 7, 156
   see also misconceptions (children's)
illnesses 39, 47, 58–9, 59–60, 61
independent variables 27–8, 29
infections 47, 58, 59–60, 61
instruments, stringed 142–3
insulators 118

Jenner, Edward (1749–1823) 20, 33
joints 66, 67, 68
Joule, James (1818–89) 120
joules 120
Jupiter 133

Lava 93–4
   law of reflection 138
leaves 39, 53, 61, 62–3
life characteristics 39, 56–8, 76
  animals 40
  plants 51
life cycles 39
  animals 42–3, 70
  plants 44–5, 71
light 39, 112, 118
  and plants 53
  reflection 112, 131–2, 132, 133, 136–8, 152
  and seeing 63–6
  and shadows 4, 112, 138–41, 153
  sources 112, 131–3
lightning flashes 117
liquids 79, 100–1
  see also water
living things 39, 56–8, 76
loudness 112, 141, 142, 154
lubrication 128

Magnetism 112, 133–6
magnifiers 59, 95, 127
mass 129, 131
materials 79
  properties 91, 112
  sorting 89–92, 109
  states of 79, 99–102
measuring
  energy 120
  forces 126
  gravity 131
  loudness 154
mechanical energy 112, 118, 119
melting 79, 84, 92–4, 102, 110
micro-organisms 39, 47, 58–61, 77

microbes 39, 47, 58–61, 77
microscopes 58, 59
mirrors 112, 132, 136–8, 152, 157
misconceptions (children's) 4, 6, 7, 156
  about electricity 115
  about energy 118
  about evaporation 86–7
  about floating and sinking 121–2
  about light sources 132
  about microbes 58
  about seeing 63–5
  about shadows 139
Montagu, Mary (Lady Mary Wortley Montagu, 1689–1762) 20, 33
Moon 131, 133
movement, animals 39, 40
musical instruments 142–3

Newtons 126
noise 141
non-living things 39, 56–8, 76
non-reversible changes 79, 80–1, 106
nutrition 39
  animals 40, 61–2
  green plants 51, 61–3

Objects, sound properties of 112
oil, lubrication with 128
once-living things 39, 56, 57

Patterns
  behavioural 15
  reflection 136
  in science 10, 13–16, 17–18, 31
  in stretching 102–3
pendulums 128
people *see* humans
permanent changes 79, 80–1, 106
permeability 79, 94–6
photosynthesis 61, 62–3
physical changes 82
pitch 112, 141, 142, 143
plants
  compared with animals 53
  green plants 51–3, 61–3, 74
  growth 44–5, 53, 71, 81
  and light 53
  nutrition 39, 61–3
  and water 53, 63, 156–7
poles, of magnets 134, 135–6
prediction 10, 13, 14, 16–18, 18, 32
  about floating 123
  about reflection 137
properties of materials 91, 112
pulls (forces) 125, 125–6, 148
pushes (forces) 125, 125–6, 148